David V. Tansley

subtle body

Essence and shadow

With 122 illustrations, 15 in colour

Thames and Hudson · London

For Daron, Donna and Denny

Art and Imagination
General Editor: Jill Purce

Printed in the Netherlands.

Contents

Open the being to God,
Abide in stillness.
Life arises, and passes,
Birth, growth, and return,
A rhythmic arc from Source to Source.
In the rhythm is quietude,
A tranquil submission;
In the soul's submission is peace,
Absorption in Eternity.
And so, the Great Light!

Lao-Tzu

All portions of the body's reality are versions in flesh of the soul's reality, even as all segments of the exterior universe mirror an internal one.

Jane Roberts

The study of the human soul lies within the province of anatomy.

Andreas Vesalius

Man – essence and shadow

One of the most persistent beliefs held by man throughout the ages is that his physical form is but the reflection of a series of subtler bodies, and that in their totality these invisible, interpenetrating forms reflect the nature of God, the Cosmic Man crucified in space upon the cross of matter.

Most, if not all, of the spiritual and philosophical writings and teachings that have emerged through the ages bear witness to this concept. It is clear that the ancient Egyptians, Chinese and Greeks, the Indians of North America, the tribes of Africa, the Polynesian Kahunas, the Incas, the early Christians, the Vedic seers of India, and the medieval alchemists and mystics of Europe, have all in one way or another seen man and the study of his anatomy, both physical and subtle, as a key to the nature of God and the universe.

One of the profoundest mystics of ancient India, Shankara, wrote in his *The Crest Jewel of Discrimination*: 'Man is more than his shadow'; and in Europe hundreds of years later the Renaissance natural philosopher Paracelsus echoed his theme, saying that if we follow the light of nature, we learn that there exists another half of man: man does not consist of flesh and blood alone, but also of a body that cannot be discerned by our crude eyesight. Man, he tells us, has bodies visible and invisible. The visionary Jacob Boehme, in his treatise, the *Aurora*, expresses the same idea more forcefully:

Open your eyes, and consider yourselves: Man is made according to the similitude, and out of the power, of God in his Ternary. Behold thy inward man, and then thou wilt see it most plainly and clearly; if thou art not a fool and an irrational beast; therefore observe.

These correlations of the nature of man and of God underlie all the philosophical and religious doctrines of the ancient world. Its traditional teachings were broadly divided into two categories: one for those who could understand only the literal expression of Nature's deeper mysteries, and who worshipped the great forces of the universe as gods and goddesses; and the other for those who were capable of looking beyond the images of the gods to the abstract truths and spiritual realities they represented. Those who found themselves in the latter group often formed schools or fraternities where instruction was given in the inner or esoteric meaning of the teachings. This esoteric content formed a body of knowledge known as the Mysteries, and its secrets were transmitted from the priests to their disciples in a language heavily veiled in symbolism, thus ensuring that only those who had deserved initiation would gain access to the powerful forces of nature and use them for the service of others. Each civilization has its own Mysteries, and many esoteric schools have flourished; among them in the west have been those of Hermes, Isis, Eleusis and Mithras, the Druids and the Rosicrucians. Through study and contemplation of the teachings, the aspirant learns how a deeper understanding of his relationship to God ultimately leads him to a state of conscious union with the Godhead.

Central to all the Mysteries is the idea that man, made in the image of God, has a threefold nature comprising spirit, soul and body. The spirit of man is seen as the true essence, the immortal seed: as a spark of the Divine

Mind and the Father in Heaven. Spirit is male in nature, and the body, made of matter, is its earthy, female opposite. When these two polar opposites come into union, their interaction gives birth to the soul. This, according to Greek tradition, is a radiant body of light, which they called *augoeides*, meaning 'form of radiance'. Damascius wrote of this body:

> In heaven, indeed, our radiant *augoeides* is full filled with heavenly radiance, a glory that streams throughout its depths, and lends it a divine strength. But in lower states, losing this radiance, it is dirtied, as it were, and becomes darker and darker and more material.

Like the mystics of all disciplines, Damascius speaks of the light of the soul as dimmed by its descent into the coarser grades of matter on its way to incarnation. The Bible uses the analogy of the shadow cast into the far country, in the parable of the prodigal son; and Plato in the *Phaedrus* says that the soul of man is imprisoned in his body like an oyster in its shell. In the *Vedas* or holy writings of India, man is spoken of as the 'honey eater'; who comes to the hive of the soul in order to partake of the divine nectar of the spirit.

The soul of man is veiled, according to the *Bhagavad Gita*, by three vestures or bodies, one of the mind, one of emotion, and one of dense physical matter. These three levels must come under the domination of the soul during its long journey back to the Father's House. The methods for bringing about this domination are outlined in the teachings of all esoteric traditions. First the disciple is admonished, 'Know Thyself', and from a theoretical outline of his true nature he moves by means of physical, emotional and mental purification, brought about by the disciplines of prayer, study and meditation, and by other austerities, to a direct perception of the soul and spirit within. Thus the disciple learns to radiate the light of the soul into the darkness of the three worlds and to overcome the restrictions of matter.

All esoteric tradition agrees that man consists of a variety of bodies that are distinct from his physical form; but there appears to be some disagreement as to the number that exist. The Kahunas, for example, divide man into three broad divisions: the lower-self; the middle-self; and the higher-self that they call *aumakua*, 'perfectly trustworthy spirit'. Each of these three aspects is then further divided into three, to which the physical body is added, giving ten elements in all. On the other hand, the teachings outlined in the Tarot speak of man as having three bodies or five or even seven. It is easy to get a confused picture of the inner nature of man if the subject is approached in a strictly intellectual manner, for much of the terminology used is in the nature of a blind, which carries revelation to those who can function intuitively but tends to perplex those who are not ready for the inner truths. It must be remembered that verbal and pictorial analogies of the subtle anatomy of man are but 'fingers pointing to the moon', to be used as guidelines but not to be confused with reality.

In *Tales of Power*, by Carlos Castaneda, the sorcerer Don Juan draws a diagram in some ashes from a fire to represent the luminous body of man, admonishing Castaneda not to think of himself as a solid body. When Castaneda points out that the diagram is not the same as the last one he

The Indian monkey god Hanuman, containing the figure of gods within his heart, symbolizes the spiritual forces held within the animal form. (Hanuman carrying Siva and Parvati in his heart, Kalighar painting, India, c. 1880, British Museum, London.)

recorded, Don Juan tells him quickly that the outer form is of no importance at all; the diagram is not a body. In other words, do not be trapped by the symbol, but look beyond and see the reality. Although a basic intellectual understanding of the subtle bodies is important, this mode of knowing must be transcended and transformed into experience; this alone turns the key to the locked door of the Mysteries and provides the student with a true knowledge of his inner being.

There are of course individuals who have clairvoyant ability to see the subtle bodies of man; but this form of perception is not open to all. Its absence should not be seen as a hindrance to investigating the inner nature of man, but rather as an incentive; for this often enables the individual to develop the higher faculty of intuitive perception which is more accurate than clairvoyance.

In *The Secret Doctrine*, Madame Blavatsky, the Theosophical teacher, quotes a passage from Buddhist teachings which is very appropriate to the study of the subtle anatomy of man:

> The Lord Buddha has said that we must not believe in a thing said merely because it is said; nor traditions because they have been handed down from antiquity; nor rumours, as such; nor writings by sages, because sages wrote them; nor fancies that we may suspect to have been inspired in us by a Deva [that is, in presumed spiritual inspiration]; nor from inferences drawn from some haphazard assumption we may have made; nor because of what seems an analogical necessity; nor on the mere authority of our teachers or masters. But we are to believe when the writing, doctrine, or saying is corroborated by our own reason and consciousness. 'For this,' says he in concluding, 'I taught you not to believe merely because you have heard, but when you believed of your consciousness, then to act accordingly and abundantly.'

Alice Bailey, who was to follow in the footsteps of Madame Blavatsky and act as amanuensis for a Tibetan Master of the Wisdom known as Djwal Khul, uses the same quotation in the foreword to *A Treatise on Cosmic Fire*, and adds that a willingness to consider the esoteric teachings with sympathy, honesty and sincerity of thought will aid in the development of intuition and spiritual discrimination. Her writings provide one of the most lucid technical outlines in existence of the subtle bodies of man.

The body-temple of man

In many traditional religious teachings the human physical form is referred to as a creation of the Divine Architect, and symbolized as a temple. The Bible, for example, speaks of man as the Holy City of Ezekiel, the tabernacle in the wilderness, or the Temples of Solomon and Zerubbabel. St Paul says: 'Know ye not that ye are the temple of the living God?' and Jesus himself said, 'Destroy this temple and in three days I will raise it up again.' The building of temples in the form of a stylized human body is a common theme in all lands. The great Egyptian temple at Karnak, the Jewish tabernacles, and the temples of India follow this form. Most Christian churches are laid out in the shape of a cross, thus reflecting the shape of the human body lying supine with arms outstretched. In the *Upanishads* the

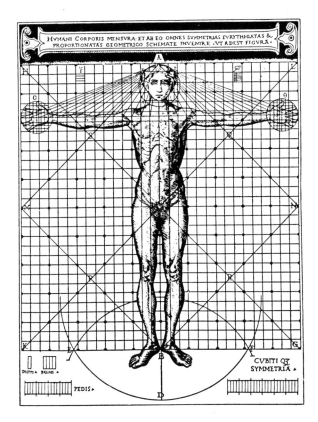

The proportions of the macrocosm, being reflected in man, were used by the initiate master masons in the buildings of temples, churches and cathedrals, thus preserving the mysteries of God in religious structures. (The human body as source of architectural proportion, after Cesariano's edition of Vitruvius, from Hall, 'Man, Grand Symbol of the Mysteries'.)

Indian seers describe the body as the City of Brahman, a heavenly, desirable dwelling in which, as in a house, the lotus flower of the heart abides. Paracelsus in a similar vein wrote that the seat of the soul is in the heart, and that the body is the house of the soul. Both eastern and western teachings say that the soul of man resides in the heart, and from this has grown the veneration of the human form as a temple wherein a god resides.

All temples of true spiritual worship have three divisions: an outer court, an inner court, and a Holy of Holies. It should be no surprise, then, that the human form has three corresponding divisions. First there is the area consisting of the abdomen, the pelvic girdle and sacrum or sacred bone, containing the viscera and organs of physical generation, corresponding to the outer court of the temple. This represents the chamber where the candidate for initiation into the Mysteries takes part in the rituals that aid him in his first significant expansion of consciousness. In this phase of his training he gains an understanding of the various aspects of thought and the correct use of the lower mind. This part of the mind is often referred to as the 'Slayer of the Real', for if it becomes overactive it detracts from the functioning of the higher or intuitive mind and may temporarily cut man off from the Source of his being.

Separated from the abdomen by the diaphragm is the box-like structure of the rib-cage. This contains the heart and lungs, organs of life and vitality. It is the Inner Court or Holy Place in Solomon's Temple. The heart is often spoken of as the chamber of initiation, perched upon the mountain-top of the diaphragm which separates the mundane worlds below from those of the soul and spirit above. Here the initiate learns of the power of the soul and its function on the plane of abstract thought.

9

The Holy of Holies is the chamber represented by the head, containing the brain and the pineal and pituitary glands, the latter long claimed by the priest-physicians to be the organs of spiritual perception. In this chamber the initiate proceeds to the third degree. The Christian mystic Meister Eckhart may well have been expressing this experience when he wrote:

> Intellect is the highest power of the soul, and therewith the soul grasps the divine good. Free will is the power of relishing the divine good which intellect makes known to it. The man of the soul, transcending his angelic mode and guided by the intellect, pierces the source whence flowed the soul. Intellect itself is left outside with all named things. So the soul is merged in pure unity.

It is at the high altar in the head that the initiate prays continually to God, for he is conscious then of the Divine Presence in all things, and his life becomes a prayer. Having penetrated the inner sanctum of the Holy of Holies and learned to express the Love and the Will of God through the linking of his head and heart, the initiate stands forth as a server of the race. He now knows the meaning of the ancient axiom: 'As a man thinketh in his heart, so is he.'

The threefold way of the spine

Linking the three courts of the body-temple is the spinal column, a most vital and significant structure from the esoteric point of view. Coiled at the base of the spine lies the serpent power, Kundalini. Blavatsky called it the fohatic or electrical power, the great pristine force which underlies all organic and inorganic matter. As the individual develops it uncoils and rises along the spine, bringing about spiritual regeneration as it rises from the realms of darkness below to the light in the spirit above. The ancient Egyptians saw the spine as the link between the upper and lower heavens, representing a vital sustaining power.

Anatomically the spine is a flexible column, consisting of thirty-three bony segments or vertebrae, the main purpose of which is to house and protect the spinal cord, the principal element in the central nervous system. The number thirty-three is thought to have a deep spiritual significance. Thirty-three was the cryptic signature of Francis Bacon, a man well versed in the Mysteries. The life span of the Master Jesus was thirty-three years; and the Psalmist David took thirty-three years to reach a state of spiritual enlightenment wherein the energies of his head, representing the spirit, had blended correctly with those of his heart, symbolizing the soul. The Bible expresses this by pointing out that David united the forces of Israel (the head) with those of Judah (the heart) before he could reign as king in Jerusalem, which is known as the City of Peace, symbolizing a balanced and integrated human being. The name David means 'Beloved of God': he who has linked his head and his heart.

Rosicrucian writings have outlined correlations between the vertebrae of the spine and the planets of our solar system. The seven cervical vertebrae, those of the neck, relate to the following planets: the first to Saturn; the second to Jupiter; the third to Mars; the fourth to the Sun; the fifth to Venus; the sixth to Mercury; and the seventh to the Moon. There are twelve dorsal or thoracic vertebrae, which are said to represent the signs of the zodiac. The five lumbar vertebrae are located in the middle of the body and form the lower part of the spine; each represents one of the five elements of Fire, Earth, Air, Water and Ether, and they come jointly under the rulership of Libra, for in this area the point of balance of the body is maintained. The five segments of the sacrum, said to contain the Kundalini power, are fused; their ruler is Scorpio. At the tip of the sacrum are the four coccygeal segments, united into one bone, thus making up the number of vertebrae to thirty-three.

The spine then represents the link between spirit (in the head) and matter (in the area of the sacrum). The threefold refining fire of the Kundalini, which regenerates man, ascends through the etheric spine under the astrological rulership of the three fiery signs. The purification begins in the Outer Court symbolized by the generative centre under Sagittarius; it rises to the heart or Inner Court under Leo, and from thence ascends to the Holy of Holies in the head under Aries. As the sacred fire rises in ever increasing volume and intensity it is said to unite with a luminous ethereal substance emanating from the blood, and the amalgamated essences then awaken the inner spiritual eye. The initiate then demonstrates the ancient maxim: 'If thine eye be single, thy whole body shall be full of light.' The light or radiance that fills man as he unites with the source of his being is depicted in religious paintings as the corona or halo around the head. This type of representation is a dominant feature of Christian art; the plumes of the serpent, in the tradition of the Indians of Mexico, symbolize this same energy field or coronal discharge around the initiate or anointed one, and the magnificent feather headdresses of the North American chiefs, flowing from the crown of the head and down the back, indicate their spiritual status and wisdom.

The spinal column is surmounted by the skull, which the anthroposophical teacher Rudolf Steiner likened to a distended vertebra. The brain is enclosed by the walls of the skull, described by Plato as an imitation of the periphic constitution of the world. The *Taittireeya Upanishad* says that where the skull divides there lies the gate of God; through it man goes forth crying into fire and air and sun and spirit, in spirit he attains heaven and conquers his mind. The skull has been spoken of as the microcosmic heaven resting on the atlas or upper vertebra of the neck; here is the intersection of horizontal and vertical, the point of crucifixion at Golgotha the place of the skull.

Anatomically the skull consists of twenty-two bones, fourteen making up the face and eight the cranium. Kabbalists suggest that this arrangement is described in the *Sepher Yetsirah*, where it is set forth how the Lord, Blessed be He, arranged the twenty-two Hebrew letters in the form of a wall. In the head are the ventricles of the brain, and these symbolize the caves or dwelling-places of the hermits and sages who have travelled along the 'sacred river' of the spine.

The heart – chamber of light

All parts of the human body are rich in symbolism, yet perhaps more than any other organ the heart has caught and held the imagination and attention of philosophers of every age and civilization. Two threads of energy are said to link the form of man to his soul. The first thread is one of consciousness, and is anchored in the head, at the pineal gland. The second, or life-thread, is anchored in the heart at the sino-auricular node, a specialized mass of tissue that governs the heartbeat; it is frequently spoken of as the pacemaker. As long as the connection of the life-thread to the heart is maintained, then man continues to live and work on the physical plane of existence. On the other hand, the consciousness-thread is severed every time the individual sleeps; this enables the ensouling life to function in other worlds during such periods. The following verses from the Vedas refer to this entry into other spaces:

> *Throwing off in sleep what pertains to the body,*
> *Sleepless he contemplates the sleeping organs;*
> *Borrowing their light he returns then back to his place,*
> *The golden spirit, the sole bird of passage.*
>
> *This lower nest he would have guarded by the life,*
> *And himself rises aloft immortal from the nest;*
> *Immortal he moves whither he will,*
> *The golden spirit, the sole bird of passage.*

Further verses point out the danger of being suddenly awakened, and the difficulty of finding a cure for one who fails to find his way back into the physical form. A sudden re-entry can create a great shock to the body, which will be left shaking violently from the impact. Those who function in full consciousness in both the sleeping and waking states can observe their own gliding return to the physical form. In the Bible the combined energies of the consciousness- and life-threads are called the silver cord. When these two aspects are simultaneously severed, death ensues, the physical body is discarded by the soul, and its constituent atoms flow back into the universal pool of substance where they will remain until drawn upon by some other individual on his return journey to physical existence.

The area of the sino-auricular node in the heart receives fibres from the vagus nerve, which is spoken of by Corinne Heline (in her *Occult Anatomy and the Bible*) as 'the Pathway for the Breath of the Holy Spirit'. When complete regeneration is accomplished by the aspirant, a powerful stream or current of energy is intuitively perceived to flow along the vagus nerve, coordinating the powers of the head and the heart.

The *Vedas* refer to the heart as the seat of Brahma or the spiritual centre of consciousness in man, and compare it with the hanging cup of a lotus flower or banana blossom. God lives in the hollow of the heart, state the *Vedas*, filling it with immortality, light and intelligence (see p. 41). In the lotus flower of the heart, they claim there is a small space containing heaven and earth, sun, moon and stars, and in it 'the lights of the universe shine enclosed'. Shankara observed that the soul is as a light, the size of the thumb, in the cavity of the heart. The *Kath Upanishad* reflects this concept:

> *An inch in height, here in the body*
> *The purusha dwells,*
> *Lord of the past and the future;*
> *He who knows him frets no more,*
> *In truth, this is that.*

Like flame without smoke, an inch in height
The purusha is in size,
Lord of the past and the future;
It is he today and also tomorrow,
In truth, this is that.

Paracelsus, the supreme physician of the Renaissance, steeped in the mystical traditions of Europe, described this 'dweller in the heart' as a bluish flame-like body, equal in size to the last joint on a man's thumb. The Taoist adepts of China likened the heart to a chamber of fire located between heaven (the head) and earth (the abdomen), and said that its transmutation led to immortality. Arab physicians of the past have claimed that if a certain point in the heart of a living animal be touched with the finger the heat is so intense as to cause a blister. In western mystic tradition the heart is the location of the Christ Light; and Jesus himself urged his disciples to enter into the silence of this chamber in order to commune directly with the Father.

If clairvoyantly observed, the point at which the life-thread is anchored in the heart shines forth as an intense violet light. Manly Palmer Hall, in *Man, Grand Symbol of the Mysteries*, states that this point of light was known to medieval theologians as the eastern part of the Garden of Eden, the heart itself being, within the body, the Paradise of Eden from which spring the rivers (arteries) through which the living waters (blood) flow out for the preservation of the land, symbol of the physical form.

Blood – the mysterious essence

For many thousands of years, since man began to question his place in the universe and his relationship to life itself, blood, the flowing essence of life, has played an important role in his search for meaning, and whole mythologies have grown around it. The scriptures of the world are filled with references to blood as the bearer of life. Physiologically it carries a continuous supply of nutrients and oxygen to all parts of the body and removes debris and waste gases and other impurities. According to the Vedic teachings the life-principle anchored in the heart of man is able to blend with the blood and thus carry the life-force or *prana* to all areas of the organism; *prana* is the name given to those energizing forces which flow from the sun. The heart, working in conjunction with the spleen, distributes these solar energies to vitalize the physical form.

The relationship between blood and life is evident. Death comes as blood leaves the body. The monthly flow of menstrual blood in the human female temporarily ceases its cyclic flow as new life in the form of a child begins to make its appearance. Blood is in a sense the essence of life; and no doubt out of this grew the belief that the power to revitalize and regenerate lies in blood sacrifice. The Greeks said that spirits gathered at sacrifices in order to absorb the life forces of the spilled blood. Such is the power present in shed blood, wrote Paracelsus, that its emanations provide enough matter to form a visible body for a discarnate entity.

Many thousands of years ago people ceremonially coated the bodies of their dead with a red mineral pigment called haematite. Haematite is a Greek word meaning 'blood-stone' and its use in burial was universal.

Graves between 20,000 and 45,000 years old, as far apart as Siberia, France, Bavaria, Wales and South Africa, all show clear evidence of the ancient belief in the life forces contained in blood and blood-stone. Both African and Australian tribesmen relate the legend of the Mother Goddess of the earth whose blood soaked into the soil to form great deposits of haematite. Even today blood-stone is used for healing purposes to stop bleeding of the lungs and uterus, as an antidote to snakebite, and to clear bloodshot eyes. It is also used as a cosmetic in Africa for ritual purposes, and similar uses were made of it by the native Americans and the ancient Chinese.

The use of blood in religious ritual has been replaced in the modern world by substitute elements. This is symbolized most clearly in the Eucharist, where the initiate partakes of the body of Christ through the wafer and of the blood of Christ through the wine, consecrated beforehand by appropriate rituals and prayer.

The Rosicrucian Max Heindel wrote that the soul controls the dense physical body by way of the blood which is its particular vehicle. Empedocles in 480 BC stated that 'blood is life', and Goethe had Faust say that man's blood is a liquid fire. Steiner spoke of the blood as containing a record of the life of the individual, registering every thought and emotion, life being transmitted from the ethers through breath to the lungs and there making its impress on the blood. All mystics agree with Jacob Boehme that the spirit of God moves in the blood of man, and everyone is familiar with the Christian phrase 'saved by the blood of Christ'. There are of course many interpretations of this, and some recognize that it can mean the reorganization of the energies within the individual as the Christ comes to birth within him.

Buddhist texts outline techniques for determining the nature of another's thoughts through the colour of his or her heart-blood: such cognition is produced by developing the power of clairvoyance in order to see the heart-blood. If a person has happy thoughts then the colour seen is red like the ripe banyan fruit; if sad thoughts then the colour is black; and if the thoughts are predominantly neutral the heart-blood appears to have the colour of clear sesamum oil.

Glands – hierarchy of equilibrium

The endocrine glands are those which secrete hormones into the blood stream to create a balance of life within the physical organism. The word 'hormone' comes from a Greek word meaning 'to arouse or set in motion'. There are seven major endocrine glands, which govern human behaviour, determine body-build and control emotional and mental attitudes; they also have a profound effect upon the nutritional and nervous systems and the general health of the individual. The endocrine glands were a special focus of study for the priest-physicians of India; they saw in them the regulators of man as a physical, moral and spiritual being (see pp. 82–83).

Five of these glands are located along the cerebro-spinal axis. The gonads are positioned at the base of the torso, and their role is to produce hormones related to sexual reproduction. Above, riding astride the kidneys, are the adrenal glands. One of their primary roles is to produce adrenalin which plays an important part in the 'fight or flight' mechanism by accelerating the heart rate and shutting off blood flow to areas like the intestines and skin, and providing the muscles with extra blood and sugar released from the liver. The ancient teachers linked these glands with the physical 'will-to-be'; and modern physiology tends to bear this concept out, for if the adrenal glands are removed death is rapid and inevitable.

The pancreas is located in the area of the solar plexus; its secretions deal with the digestive processes, and it directs the liver to release stored sugar into the blood stream to provide the organism with heat and energy.

Above the diaphragm and beneath the breastbone lies the thymus. Its important relationship to the life-thread anchored in the heart was not overlooked by physicians of past civilizations; modern medicine, however, has seen no reason to include this gland in the endocrine hierarchy until recently. Its role in immune reactions has now been noted, and it is thought that it might work with the adrenals in dealing with stress situations. As a result of these findings it is rather grudgingly admitted that the thymus may be endocrine in nature.

The thyroid lies at the base of the throat, wrapped around the windpipe. Its hormones affect the whole body and have a very profound effect upon metabolism. The ancients saw this gland as the focal point for the higher creative energies in man, the polar opposite of the gonads. A deficiency of thyroid hormone produces a stunted, dull individual devoid of intelligence. Embedded in the thyroid are the tiny glands known as the parathyroids. They are essential to life and play a vital role in controlling the calcium and phosphorus balance in the body.

Contained within the head are the pineal and pituitary glands (see pp. 56–57). The pineal is not fully recognized by medical science as a hormone-producing gland; but, like the thymus, it is beginning to have some mention in texts on endocrinology. The pineal is located under the cerebrum and fairly close to the cerebellum, and has been found to contain vestigial traces of optic tissue. Experiments have shown that nerve impulses arise in the pineal in response to stimulation by light. Galen claimed that the pineal was a regulator of thought, and the Greeks said that the soul was anchored there. According to esoteric tradition this gland is the focal point for the masculine, positive energy of spirit which is represented by the first hexagram of the *I Ching*, its six yang lines symbolizing the primal power of heaven and the creative action of the holy man.

Located behind and below the bridge of the nose is the pituitary gland. This gland is the controller, the conductor of the endocrine orchestra. When the bloodstream contains the correct amount of each hormone from each gland, the pituitary remains at rest, but if for example there is a deficiency of secretion from one gland, the pituitary will elaborate what is called a tropic hormone and this will enter the blood stream, home in on the underactive gland, and stimulate its action, thus maintaining the proper balance.

If the pituitary is overactive, it stimulates a dynamic and magnetic personality; normally such people are very successful in business and work with great enthusiasm. From this point the lower-self can function with great power. Here, the ancients claimed, man gathers all the energies of his personality or lower-self in preparation for their union with the spirit in the area of the pineal. Goethe experienced this gathering of energies when he said: 'My whole being is concentrated between my eyebrows.' Thus the

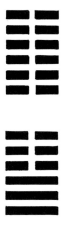

forces of the feminine, earthy, principle represented by the second hexagram of the *I Ching*, The Receptive, prepare to submit to the positive, dominant energies of the spirit.

The pineal and the pituitary have been likened to the male and female reproductive organs because of the similarity of structure. In Taoist texts they are frequently depicted as the tiger and the dragon, 'copulating' in the alchemical cauldron of the brain, bringing about the oneness of heaven and earth and giving rise to the eleventh hexagram of Peace and a time of universal flowering and prosperity. Christ the Prince of Peace now rules his Temple, when the Sun symbolizing the spirit has obliterated the light of the Moon representing the forces of the lower nature. St John said of this: 'He must become more and I must become less.' This experience, according to Teilhard de Chardin, is a 'grievous hour' for our lower nature; but there emerges a man who has undergone the deepest spiritual illumination, one who has passed a major milestone on his return to the Father's House.

According to Alice Bailey, the three aspects of Deity work through the glandular system: Will functioning through the pineal, Love through the thymus and Active Intelligence through the thyroid. There is a curious parallel here between the spiritual status of man and the degree of our scientific understanding of these three glands. Certainly there is overwhelming physiological evidence that intelligence as we know it is related to thyroid function: the intelligence of man is well developed, which is why so much is known to science about the gland which is the centre of its activity. However, the aspect of Love is in the process of unfoldment; and the spiritual Will in man is relatively quiescent. On this basis it can be predicted that, as man learns to express Love and his spiritual Will, so more knowledge will come to light regarding the functions of the thymus and pineal glands.

The Rosicrucian teachings refer to the endocrine glands as the 'Invisible Guardians', recognizing that they are the controllers and guardians of life who determine the equilibrium of the spiritual and more physical forces in man. Each gland has certain spiritual correspondences which become clearer as the force centres that govern them are studied. These centres are represented by the seven roses on the Rosy Cross of the Rosicrucian Order, and through them the spirit of man finally gains control and dominion of the more physical aspects of his nature.

Descent of spirit into matter

Madame Blavatsky wrote that matter is spirit at its lowest level, and spirit is matter at its highest level. Theosophical teaching further contends that the spirit of man occultly died and sacrificed itself to descend into matter in order to learn to to overcome the limitations of the lower-self and in so doing redeem matter and 'raise it up into heaven'. The spirit or immortal part of man is referred to as a spark of the universal mind; the Indians call it Brahman, the supreme principle, and the Egyptian priests named it Za. In the writings of Alice Bailey this inner spark is known as the Monad; and Teilhard de Chardin frequently uses this same term in his own discourses. The nature of the Monad is recorded in the *Upanishads*:

As unity we must regard him,
Imperishable, unchanging,
Eternal, not becoming, not ageing,
Exalted above space, the great Self.

Boehme, too, saw the spirit of man as an angelic being which had sacrificed itself by leaving the Father's House in order to bring light into the darkness of matter, facing the stupendous task of helping to resolve the body of God into light, thus playing its role in releasing God from the bondage of form.

In their teachings the ancients always considered man in his relationship to God, the universal field of energy. If matter and spirit are polar opposite levels, then it is implied that there are other levels in between, reflecting a gradual transition from one state to the other, and that these levels or planes of energy are the Divine Field in which man manifests (see pp. 80–81). Boehme, like St John, writes of a sevenfold structure and the 'seven spirits of God'. The traditional Indian teachings speak also of these levels, and the Kabbalistic *Sepher Yetsirah* says:

> These Seven Double Letters He designed produced and combined and formed with them the planets of this Universe, the Days of the Week, and the Gates of the Soul in man. From these Seven He hath produced the Seven Heavens, the Seven Earths, the Seven Sabbaths; for this cause He has loved and blessed the number Seven, more than all things under Heaven.

Madame Blavatsky and Alice Bailey list these same seven planes of energy in the following manner: the highest plane is the plane of Adi; the next the Monadic; then the Atmic; then the Buddhic which is the plane of the Christ principle. Below that lie the three worlds spoken of in the *Bhagavad Gita*: the Mental plane, which is divided into the abstract, upon which the soul of man is found, and the lower concrete, from which the rational and discriminative thought processes arise; the Astral or emotional plane; and finally the Physical plane, which like the mental is divided into two aspects, the upper divisions of which are the etheric levels and the lower the dense physical plane upon which the human form appears.

Each of these seven planes of energy is further divided into seven subplanes, numbering forty-nine in all. In their totality these seven vast planes represent the Cosmic Physical Plane or the lowest physical aspect of the Being we live and move within (see p. 37). Upon these planes the three-fold man comes into manifestation, a Son of Wisdom formed from the 'Electrical fire' of spirit, the 'Solar fire' of the soul and the 'fire by friction' of the body. When the fire of the body blends with that of the soul and their combined flame with that of the spirit, the three fires blaze forth as one, and the spiritual man achieves liberation from matter.

In order to descend into matter, the spirit appropriates a series of five stable force centres, called by Alice Bailey permanent atoms; the Rosicrucian teachings refer to them as seed atoms. Like data memorybanks they hold the sublimated essence of the experiences of all past lives, determining the quality of each body as well as the nature of the life experience for any particular incarnation. These seed atoms, say the

Rosicrucians, are man's Book of Destiny, the arbiters of his fate during physical incarnation as well as in those periods spent on the inner planes of existence. The cohesive power of the Love aspect of the spirit governs the seed atoms, while the ordinary atoms of the various bodies are vitalized by the Intelligence aspect.

The Monad or spirit sounds forth its note and calls the Atmic, Buddhic and Manasic permanent atoms into activity; around each of these is formed a body on the appropriate level of consciousness. As the Bible says: 'God giveth it a body as it hath pleased him, and to every seed his own body' (I Corinthians 15:38). The linking of these three seed atoms creates a form which Alice Bailey refers to as the 'spiritual triad', and the spirit of man thus Begins its descent and is now in a position to create on the higher levels of the mental plane that body of light known as the soul which will serve as an outpost of consciousness for innumerable incarnations to come.

The *Bhagavad Gita* gives a series of practical descriptions of the subtle bodies of man:

> The Supreme Spirit, here in the body, is called the Beholder, the Thinker, the Upholder, the Taster, the Lord, the Highest Self.
>
> Illuminated by the power that dwells in all the senses, yet free from all sense-powers, detached, all-supporting, not divided into powers, yet enjoying all powers.
>
> Without and within all beings, motionless, yet moving, not to be perceived is That, because of its subtlety, That stands afar, yet close at hand.
>
> These temporal bodies are declared to belong to the eternal Lord of the body, imperishable, immeasurable.
>
> They say the sense-powers are higher than objects; than the sense-powers, emotion is higher; than emotion, understanding is higher; but higher than understanding is He.

The first two paragraphs deal with the spirit of man. The third speaks of the soul, the word 'That' frequently being used in Vedic teachings to denote the soul or power of the soul. The fourth and fifth paragraphs deal with the lower-self, 'sense powers' referring to the physical form, 'emotion' to the astral body and 'understanding' to the mental body. Higher of course than all of these is He, the soul in man. This theme is carried a little further elsewhere in the *Gita*:

> As the one Sun illumines all this world so He that abideth in the body lights up the whole field.
>
> They, who with the eye of Wisdom perceive the distinction between the field and the Knower of the field and the liberation of being from nature, go to the Supreme.

Here the lower-self in the three worlds is defined as the field, and the Knower is the soul; spiritual perception based on knowledge is the method by which man untangles himself from the snares of illusion and knows himself to be the undying one.

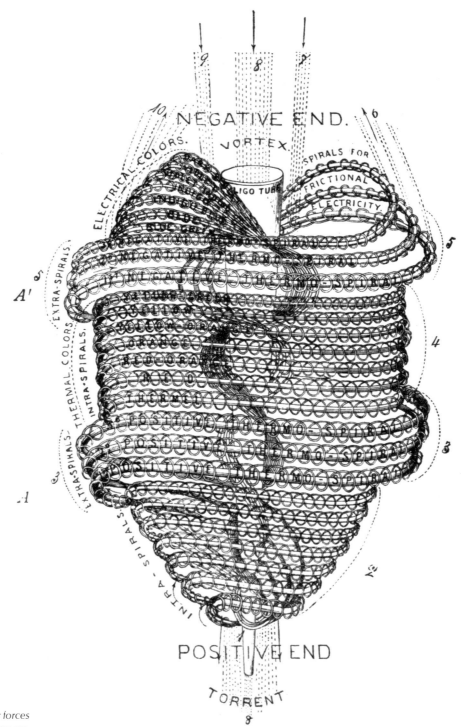

The atom receives solar forces through the vortex. These are circulated through the spirillae and appear as hues of red, blue, orange, yellow, violet and indigo. The mental body of man is similarly shaped by the cosmic forces pouring through him, and the colour flow through his aura is likewise a continuously changing display. (Babbitt, 'Principles of Light and Colour'.)

The radiant body

The soul of man is truly produced out of that which is above (spirit) and that which is below (matter). Boehme, whose spiritual vision provides one of the most detailed outlines of the subtle anatomy of man outside the Indian teachings, expresses it so:

> The soul hath its origin, not only from the body, though it taketh its rise in the body, and has its first beginning in the body; yet it hath also its source from without, by and from the air; and so the Holy Ghost ruleth in it, in that manner as he replenisheth and filleth all things.

The soul has always been spoken of in terms of radiance and light. The Indian teachings refer to it as a lotus blossom (see pp. 39, 88–89), containing a central point of energy where it is directly connected to the spirit by a fine thread, the silver cord, also called the Sutratma, upon which the permanent atoms are strung 'like pearls on a necklace'. The central point of light or fire is called the 'Jewel in the Heart of the Lotus'. As Boehme says: 'The soul containeth the first principle'; and an ancient commentary states this concept in the words: 'The Lord of Life himself sits at the heart and watches.'

The soul arises out of the interaction of spirit with the matter of the abstract levels of the mental plane, producing a series of whorls or vortices which Alice Bailey's Master, Djwal Khul, describes as a nine-petalled lotus. The action of the central point of electrical fire creates a further three petals which enfold the Jewel like a bud and shield its radiance from sight, thus making twelve petals in all. He goes on to say that the soul may be viewed as nine vibrations flowing out from a central point, pursuing a diagonal path until they reach the periphery of the soul's sphere of influence, at which point they swing around to form the spheroidal shape of the causal body. It may also be seen as nine spokes of a wheel converging to a central hub which hides the generator of all activity.

The nine petals are arranged in circles of three petals each, the petals of knowledge, love and will. When the individual soul first steps upon the path of descent into matter, these petals are in a quiescent state and virtually colourless, but during the process of successive incarnations they gradually become activated by the feedback of energies flowing through the lower-self on the mental, emotional and physical planes. First the three petals of knowledge are activated, organized and vitalized. This is carried out in the 'Hall of Ignorance', which is that phase of experience corresponding to the Outer Court wherein life is physically oriented. As the individual evolves and becomes truly Self-conscious the love petals are energized in the 'Hall of Learning' or Inner Court, and it is during this period that the aspirant to wisdom begins to make a more deliberate and sustained effort to spiritualize his lower nature. Last to become vitalized are the petals of will, or of sacrifice. This occurs in the 'Hall of Wisdom', or Holy of Holies. These unfoldings do not occur as separate and distinct occurrences but overlap each other; the completion of each is marked by one of three initiations in the three courts of the temple.

From a dull colourless ovoid the nine-petalled lotus and 'causal body' of the soul gradually assumes more brilliance and colour. The fundamental colour of the petals, to clairvoyant sight, is orange, with iridescent green, violet, rose, blue, yellow, and indigo. Reference to this is found in the

Chhandogya Upanishad:

> Orange, blue, yellow, red are not less in men's arteries than in the sun.
>
> As a long highway passes between two villages, one at either end, so the sun's rays pass between this world and the world beyond. They flow from the sun, enter into the arteries, flow back from the arteries, enter into the sun.

The circular mandala form of the soul is an archetypal shape found in all teachings. Black Elk of the Oglala Sioux said in our time that everything the power of the world does is done in a circle, and Paracelsus some four hundred years before had said:

> Everything that man accomplishes or does, that he teaches or wants to learn, must have its right proportion; it must follow its own line and remain within its circle, to the end that a balance be preserved, that there be no crooked thing, that nothing exceed the circle.

The power of the mandala was well known to the ancient teachers, and its use came to the fore in Buddhist practices, particularly those carried out in Tibet. The circle drawn upon the ground in certain magic rituals serves as a protection against the elemental forces that are being invoked. The white magician in the service of Christ stands within the circle of dynamic power which radiates from the lotus of his soul and needs no external paraphernalia to aid him in his work.

The Indians of North America speak of life as a circle flowing from childhood to childhood, and the Eskimos say that when a man dies it is not the end, but he awakes to consciousness again and returns to life, and that his rebirth is effected through the soul, which they regard as the greatest and most incomprehensible of all things.

Similarly, the Karanga and Mashona people of Rhodesia believe that man has, apart from his body which they call a shadow, another body which is invisible to ordinary sight. This is known as the *mwega*, soul or white shadow. It leaves the body at death and can also leave during sleep or trance states: it has senses of its own which are far more powerful than those of the physical body.

Forms and fields

The soul, having been established as the vehicle of manifestation for the spirit, must in its turn create a series of forms that will enable it to gain experience in the lower and denser levels of matter and consciousness. The soul comes into incarnation along the curve of descent. Dag Hammarskjöld must have intuited this delicate process when he wrote this poem called 'Single Form':

> *The breaking wave*
> *And the muscle as it contracts*
> *Obey the same law.*
>
> *An austere line*
> *Gathers the body's play of strength*
> *In a bold balance.*

Shall my soul meet
This curve, as a bend in the road
On her way to form?

The action of coming into physical incarnation involves the soul in a process similar to that carried out by the spirit. It activates the mental, astral and physical 'seed atoms'; they then draw around themselves matter from the lower mental, astral, and etheric and physical planes, forming bodies on each of these levels of consciousness, which are held together as a functional unit by the higher power of the soul.

If the soul does not hold a precise thought-form, if its attention wavers from the task of building the vehicles of the lower-self, then a stillbirth occurs, because the soul has withdrawn its consciousness to its own level. If a deep, clearly sustained thought-form is held then a child is born. The coherency and life of the forms lies in the activity of the soul, not in the bodies themselves. Over the years the soul increases its hold on the forms it has sent forth. At approximately seven years of age the *physical* form is securely anchored to earth, and the pineal gland, related to the expression of the spiritual will-to-be, atrophies. At about fourteen puberty occurs; this event signals the soul's grasp upon the *astral* body, which in many cases produces a crisis of some kind in the life of the child. At this point the thymus gland begins to atrophy. By twenty-one the *mental* body has been appropriated by the soul, an action which can in its turn bring about a crisis in the life of the individual, often resulting in much soul-searching. The inner life is of course a series of crisis-points, which very often occur in seven-year cycles. At twenty-eight work goes forward that prepares the way for the work of the soul in later years. Until thirty-five many loose ends and experiences from past lives are drawn together, and much work is put in to harmonize the will of the personality with the will of the soul. At forty-two the soul's purpose for that life should have been recognized, even if unconsciously, and the process of carrying out the work implemented.

The mental body (see p. 42) is formed from matter of the mental plane. This mechanism is used for rational, discriminative and intellectual thinking processes. To clairvoyant sight it appears as an ovoid field, the size of which depends on the mental capacity of the individual. In this field thoughts give rise to geometric patterns of colour which circulate within the ovoid. If a person's thinking is clear and concise, then the colours of the circulating forms are brilliant and precise; if on the other hand his thinking is indecisive, his mental body becomes cluttered with drab colours and displeasing shapes. This mental debris clouds his capacity to think things through in a proper manner, and serves to block off the light of the soul. The yoga techniques of stilling and controlling the mind are the means by which this body is purified, and during this process the aspirant comes to realize that many of the thoughts that appear to arise in his mind do in fact intrude from the minds of others. Through the process of observation and discrimination he is eventually able to distinguish the source of each thought that arises in the field of his mind, and to take those thoughts which are constructive and beneficent, energize them more fully and precipitate them in such a way that they will serve his fellow man. Ultimately the mental body becomes so clear and potent that it will attract only good thoughts and repel automatically those which are destructive.

The astral body is derived from the coarser matter of the astral plane. In this body the individual experiences the interplay of emotions and feels the pleasures and pains of life. The astral body connects the mind by way of the etheric body to the external world; and through this connection sensations arising in the physical world are transmitted to the mind. The astral body of an undeveloped individual is coarse in texture and dull in colour, its outlines ill defined. On the other hand a person who leads an active intellectual and spiritual life normally has an astral body that is clear and filled with luminous colours. The forms circulating in this field are the emotional aspects of the thinking processes; so the clarity of the astral field depends in part upon the nature of the thought processes and also upon the purity of the physical body itself. It is through the astral body that we sense the mood of another person or the 'atmosphere' in a room or location. So sensitive is this body to such emanations that some individuals can detect, in the form of 'astral matter', events which have taken place perhaps many hundreds of years before.

Between the astral and physical bodies lies the etheric body. This vehicle is frequently referred to as the etheric double, because its shape is similar to that of the physical form. The etheric body is composed of material drawn from the 'four ethers', the subtle aspect of the physical plane; it underlies and interpenetrates every atom, molecule and cell of the physical body, and is directly related to the nervous system which it feeds, controls and galvanizes into action. To clairvoyant sight it appears as a fine network or web of energy streams. Don Juan described it to Castaneda as fibres of light looking like white cobwebs, luminous and bristling out in all directions, putting man in touch with all things. These millions of energy fibres, to which the Indian sages gave the name of nadis, form the archetypal pattern or framework upon which the physical body is built. Paracelsus wrote of this etheric framework as the sidereal body:

> Hence man has also an animal body and a sidereal body; and both are one, and are not separated. The relation between the two is as follows. The animal body, the body of flesh and blood, is in itself always dead. Only through the action of the sidereal body does the motion of life come into the other body. The sidereal body is fire and air, but it is also bound to the animal life of man. Thus mortal man consists of water, earth, fire and air.

The etheric body has three basic functions, which are all closely related. It acts as a receiver, assimilator and transmitter of prana. Prana is the universal life force that vitalizes all forms in all kingdoms of nature. These energies streaming in from the sun are absorbed by the etheric body through a series of small force centres and then passed on to the spleen, where the vital essence of the sun is subjected to a process of intensification or devitalization, according to the condition of the organism, before being circulated to vitalize the physical body. The etheric body of man has therefore been described as negative or receptive in respect to solar radiations, and as positive or expulsive in respect to the physical body.

The astral or emotional body is
usually the most difficult to bring
under control, but ultimately it
becomes a reflector for the energies emanating from the Buddhic vehicle on the plane of
Christ-consciousness. (M., 'The
Dayspring of Youth'.)

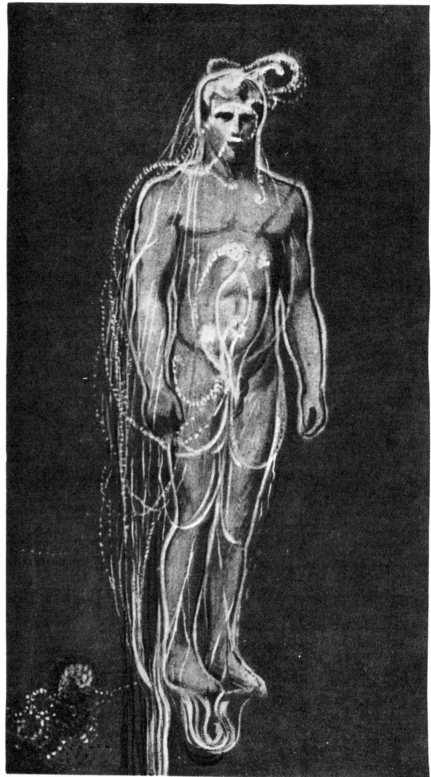

An illustration showing some of
the nadis and the major spinal
chakras. Several nadis are shown
terminating in small chakras in the
palms of the hands which may be
used in healing work. (Diagram of
the chakras and nadis in the subtle
body, India, Ajit Mookerjee Collection, New Delhi.)

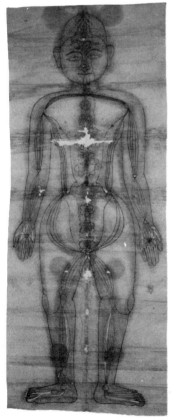

Wilhelm Reich spoke of this life force or *prana* as orgone energy, and expressed the belief that all life, from an atom to a planet, depended upon it to maintain the integrity of its form. On a clear sunny day it is possible to see the orgone dots against the blue sky, whirling and spinning in a silent dance, appearing and disappearing in a display of electrical white light. These dots correspond in detail to the vitality globules of theosophical literature, which enter the spleen to vitalize the physical body. Shankara said that breathing, circulation of the blood and nourishment, equally with quickening of the body, were the function of *prana*.

Annie Besant emphasizes in her book *Man and his Bodies* that the powers of thought and feeling and movement do not reside in the etheric or physical bodies but are activities of the soul working through these bodies by the force of *prana* as it runs along the nerve pathways. *Prana*, then, is the active energy of the self.

Good health depends upon the correct functioning of the etheric body, and this vehicle can be refined through the life forces contained in a correct diet with the emphasis upon fruit, vegetables, nuts, juices, honey and water. Devitalized foods, smoking and alcohol only serve to clog the nadis or channels and eventually create poor health. Exercise and fresh air, combined with correct breathing, also serve to cleanse the etheric body, and right thinking has an important role to play. It is responsible for the right functioning of the five senses, and thus provides five major points of contact with the outer world; it also enables man to register the inner worlds and to come into conscious contact with his soul.

When clairvoyantly observed, three main currents of energy are seen circulating in the etheric body. One runs vertically along the cerebro-spinal axis; this induces other currents of energy which appear to circulate horizontally and these in turn induce yet more currents to circulate, once more vertically. The vertical flow relates to autonomic regulation, and the horizontal current absorbs and carries vitality from the atmosphere and disposes of etheric waste products.

The word 'aura' comes from the Greek word *avra*, which means breeze. The auric fields of the astral and mental bodies extend much further from the physical body than that of the etheric, which stands out no more than a half-inch or so. The undulating flow and rhythmically shimmering colour of the mental and astral fields do give the impression that they are moved by a breeze. Perhaps the best analogy that can be given of this constantly shifting display of colour is the phenomenon of the *aurora borealis*, the Northern Lights which flicker and blaze forth in great sheets and columns of colour over the top of the world. This analogy is far more accurate than would appear at first sight, and for this reason. The sun has always symbolized the soul in man, and the earth his lower bodies of manifestation. The *aurora* occurs when solar winds bring electrons and protons into the earth's atmosphere and magnetic fields, where they collide with nitrogen and oxygen molecules, causing colour displays of breathtaking beauty. In a human being, when the activity of the soul is intensified, perhaps during prayer or meditation or in moments of intense spiritual inspiration, the energies of the soul (or solar angel as it is sometimes called) pour through the fields of the mental, astral and etheric bodies, increasing their size and the brilliance of their colours.

Chakras – gateways of consciousness

The union of spirit and matter manifests as consciousness. The soul as consciousness pervades and holds its bodies of manifestation together as a cohesive, functional unit through certain focal points. In the Indian tradition these points or centres of force are called chakras; the word in Sanskrit means 'wheel'. To clairvoyant sight they appear as wheel-like vortices of energy containing mental, astral and etheric matter. In a person of high spiritual development they are seen to revolve at great speed, and eventually to become spheres of radiant energy. They become, as the Bible puts it, 'as wheels turning within wheels'. In those of lesser spiritual development the centres are not so active, giving the impression of saucer-like depressions on the surface of the etheric body. The chakras (see pp. 80–83) are often called lotuses, each petal representing certain constituent energies. The Rosicrucians use the seven roses to symbolize these same centres of force.

Just as there is apparent disagreement in the various Mystery teachings about the number of bodies that man has, so there is some variance in the number of chakras to be found in these bodies. Tibetan writings often speak of six centres of force; others mention eight, ten or even twelve. Ancient Taoist texts show direct correspondences to the Tibetan outline of six centres, while other Chinese yoga and medical writings contain diagrams showing as many as thirty centres along the spine and twenty-four down the front of the torso.

The Theosophist C. W. Leadbeater places the chakras on the front of the body; and Gichtel, who was a disciple of Boehme, gives them a similar position. On the other hand, Tibetan and Indian literature on the subject places them along the cerebro-spinal axis (see p. 36), and the Master Djwal Khul says that they lie some three inches behind the spinal column. St John in Revelation writes of the seven seals upon the back of the book of life, which refers to these centres of force and their placement. The reason for these completely opposite views regarding the locations of the chakras is to be found in an understanding of the nature of those energies a person uses to function clairvoyantly. If he is an astral psychic he will tend to work with certain astral involutionary energies, which will predispose him to seeing the chakras as located on the front of the torso. If he is a mental psychic, then he works in matter of more rarified quality which is evolutionary in nature, and his inner vision will show him that the centres lie along the spine. Viewed symbolically, the involutionary forces in man flow from the head down the front of the torso to the pubic area, and the evolutionary forces flow up the spine from the sacrum to the head. Clearly it is essential that the aspirant to wisdom confine his attention to the ascending flow of energies, thus identifying himself with the gateways that lead upward to fusion with the soul on the higher mental plane.

The chakras have been spoken of as the focalization, or multi-concentric manifestation in space, of the dynamic life-principle. God then is seen as a series of interpenetrating concentric fields, and man as the microcosm reflects this pattern. Boehme writes of this in his *Aurora*:

Now this wheel hath seven wheels one in another, and one nave, which fitteth itself to all the seven wheels, and all the seven wheels turn on that one nave: Thus God is one God, with seven qualifying or fountain spirits one in another, where always one generateth the others, and yet is but one God, just as these seven wheels are but one wheel.

His words suggest that there are seven centres of force, and that these lie along the nave or axis of the spine. The Kabbalists said there are seven gates of the soul in man, and in more modern times C. G. Jung commented that the chakras were the gateways of consciousness in man, receptive points for the inflow of energies from the cosmos and the spirit and soul of man.

The first gate is the Muladhara, or base chakra, situated at the region of the apex of the sacrum. It externalizes as the physical body's adrenal glands, and governs the functioning of the kidneys and spinal column. The Vedic seers claimed that this centre channelled the energies of the physical will-to-be into the organism.

Above, located at the base of the lumbar spine, lies the Svadhisthana or sacral chakra. It externalizes as the gonads and governs the activity of the entire reproductive system.

The Manipura or solar-plexus chakra is located just below the level of the shoulder-blades and the diaphragm. Its glandular counterpart is the pancreas, and it governs the action of the stomach, liver, gall bladder and certain aspects of the nervous system. This centre is considered to be the great clearing-house for all of the energies below the diaphragm before they are transferred to the appropriate centres above.

The fourth centre is the Anhata or heart chakra, located between the shoulder blades; its glandular counterpart is the thymus. It governs the heart, blood and circulatory system and has a strong influence upon the vagus nerve. Through this centre man learns to radiate the energies of love flowing from the soul, out into the world he inhabits.

The Vishuddha or throat chakra is located in the region of the first dorsal vertebra at the base of the neck. Its focal point of activity is the thyroid gland, and it governs the lungs, the vocal and bronchial apparatus and the alimentary canal. Through this chakra the higher creative faculties of man are expressed.

Of the two centres in the head, the Ajna or brow chakra is located on the forehead and externalizes as the pituitary gland. The double multiple petals of the lotus symbolizing this centre represent the anterior and posterior lobes of the pituitary. Primarily it governs the lower brain and nervous system, ears, nose and the left eye which is the eye of the personality or lower-self. The Ajna centre expresses idealism and imagination.

The Sahasrara or crown chakra is at the top of the head. Its glandular expression is the pineal, the focal point for the spiritual will-to-be. It governs the upper brain and right eye. Contained within the crown centre are counterparts of all of the seven major chakras; perhaps this is what Boehme meant when he said the seven wheels were but one wheel, or Meister Eckhart when he wrote: 'In his upper member man has an image of God, which shines there without pause.'

The Ajna centre is frequently related to what is called the third or heavenly eye, and in some instances this claim is made for the pineal with its rudimentary optic tissue. It would seem that the third eye comes into being when the energy fields or auras of the pineal and pituitary glands blend harmoniously. When this occurs, the soul has a direct avenue of perception into the three worlds and is not dependent upon the often distorted feedback coming through the five physical senses. The soul in its turn eventually becomes the third eye for the Monad; and then spirit itself has an undistorted view of the worlds in which its shadow moves.

Healing and dynamic balance

Nearly 2500 years ago, Hippocrates the Greek physician took steps that were to separate the art of healing from the other sciences of the temple. He based his approach on observable facts in nature and steered the physicians of his day away from a system of healing that had become cluttered with a great deal of superstitious practice. In effect he initiated a materialistic approach to healing, a move which was to lay the foundations of modern medicine.

Today, despite the dominance of orthodox traditions derived ultimately from Hippocrates, an ever-increasing interest is being shown in those older approaches to healing (see pp. 66–71) that have come down through the ages: methods such as acupuncture, herbalism, massage, the laying-on of hands, spiritual healing and spinal manipulation (which along with surgery was banned by Papal decree in the Dark Ages). All these so-called unorthodox approaches to healing have a number of things in common; first, they are concerned with treating the causes of disease and not simply eliminating or covering up symptom patterns; second, their primary aim is to balance the energy systems of the body by means which recognize that man is more than a physical being. Their approach is to heal the total man and bring him into harmony with the universe in which he lives.

One of the oldest systems of healing in use today is acupuncture, which evolved in China several thousand years ago. The Chinese healers said that the two great forces that ruled heaven and earth also ruled man. These forces were called Yin and Yang: when they were in equilibrium man enjoyed good health; any lack of harmony between them and he became diseased. All of the organs of the body were classified as Yin or Yang organs, and were kept in a proper state of health by an energy known as *ki* or life-force. This energy circulates from one organ to another and also through specific energy pathways called meridians. Along the meridians are the acupuncture points which can be stimulated or sedated in order to balance the energy systems of the internal organs. This is done with fine needles which are inserted into the point to a particular depth and then manipulated. These points can also be treated by applied heat or simply by finger pressure. Treatment is designed to bring about a free unimpeded circulation of *ki* energy, and to enable the body to receive this energy from the cosmos. *Ki* may well be the same energy as *prana*, which is received by the chakras according to the Indian priests; if so the acupuncture points are an intricate network of tiny chakras which receive and distribute energy to the organism from the surrounding universal energy field.

Despite the apparent physicality of the technique of spinal manipulation, this too has a very profound effect upon balancing the energy fields of man. The major chakras are along the spine, and any distortion or imbalance in the vertebral column will disturb the proper functioning of the chakras, so that they will not be able to receive or distribute energies correctly. Djwal Khul says, in Alice Bailey's *Treatise on Cosmic Fire*, that the physician of the future will concern himself with two basic factors when dealing with disease. One is to see that there is correct alignment of the spine; for the spine is central to man's physical form as well as to his spiritual development. The other is to implement decongestion of the spleen, so that the latent fires of the body may blend properly with the incoming pranic forces from the sun (see p. 40). In principle this is the same aim as that of the acupuncturist, that of balancing energy circulation; only the method of obtaining this balance is different. Massage, frequently used as an adjunct to spinal manipulation, is also a very useful method of balancing the energies in man, particularly if the practitioner is aware that his hands are immersed in the etheric body of the patient as he works.

Perhaps even older than acupuncture and manipulation are those methods of healing which involve prayer and the laying-on of hands. These techniques, to be effective, require that the healer has the capacity to contact those higher forces and to channel them properly on behalf of the patient. He must be able to call upon the healing power of his own soul and to act as a catalyst in the healing process, remaining untouched and not overstimulated in any way by the forces that pour through him to the patient. In the laying-on of hands a variety of techniques may be used. In some cases the healer may simply place his hands over the diseased area and mentally direct the energies into it; often a feeling of warmth occurs when this is done. At other times, if the healer is able to work in this manner, he will link his heart chakra with his soul, and invoke its energies to flow down into the heart, and then transfer the flow to the Ajna chakra. The right hand is then placed over the chakra in the patient's body which governs the area where the disease is located, and the left hand is placed facing it on the other side of the body. The energies are then directed from the Ajna centre through the minor chakras in the hands. The healing continues for as long as the practitioner can hold the link between his centres and the soul. Finally when the healing is completed the energies are returned from the Ajna to the soul, thus completing the triangular flow required in this approach.

The hands can be used to scan the auras of the patient and to detect the chakras and their functional capacity. This method of diagnosis is used by quite a number of healers to determine the areas of imbalance in the various subtle bodies of their patients. Treatment is applied with the hands also, by mentally directing energy through them to the areas of imbalance without actually touching the physical body. It is possible to scan a person with the hands no matter how far he or she may be from the practitioner. If this is done with the eyes closed, in quiet surroundings, visual images of the areas of imbalance will arise in the mind; they can then be treated and the changes taking place observed in the same manner.

The healer of the future will no doubt have an extensive knowledge of the subtle bodies of man and the energies that can be utilized to bring balance to them. To this he will add a detailed knowledge of physical anatomy, physiology and pathology, thus ensuring that he is qualified in both the esoteric and orthodox fields. Certainly he will have to function consciously as a soul, thus taking full responsibility for what he does as he seeks to heal those who come to him for help.

There are today a growing number of medical doctors, chiropractors and osteopaths who have the capacity to see and scan the energy fields of their

The energy of the soul can be used to heal if the healer has the ability to create and utilize the links of energy illustrated in the diagram. To do so requires the capacity to visualize the linking process clearly and then to hold the image one-pointedly until the healing work is finished. (Bailey, 'Esoteric Healing'.)

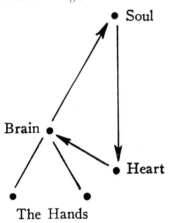

patients in the manner described. In Japan electronic instrumentation has been developed that feeds the electrical impulses from the acupuncture meridians through a computer which gives a printed diagnostic read-out. This is correlated with data obtained from another instrument called a chakra scanner, and a complete picture of the patient's health is obtained in terms of energy readings.

In 1935 Northrop and Burr put forward their theory of the electro-dynamic basis of life, saying that all life forms were controlled and maintained by an underlying electro-dynamic field. Burr called this the L (Life) field, and in his experimental work demonstrated that the electro-dynamic field of man could be measured for diagnostic purposes in both physical and psychiatric medicine. He likened the L field to a mould which held the molecules and cells of the body in a recognizable form, and vitalized it so that the organism functioned. His description of the L field tallies very closely with the Vedic concept of the etheric body, and measurements made with a vacuum tube voltmeter clearly show the dramatic effect of one individual's electro-dynamic field upon that of another. Burr said that soon every physician will have a voltmeter, because it will be recognized in the healing arts that the source of disease and imbalance lies first and foremost in the energy fields of man, and that for purposes of accurate diagnosis these fields will have to be measured. Perhaps then more credence will be given to the existence of the subtle bodies of man, as described by the seers and healers of the past, and we shall see a general return of spiritual values into the field of medicine.

Meditation – the inner ascent

The disciplines of prayer, contemplation and meditation are the means by which man ascends through ever expanding and ever more refined spheres of consciousness, to a state of union with the Godhead that lies at the core of his being. Many are the techniques that have evolved for accomplishing this task, and it is clear that a knowledge of man's esoteric constitution is to some degree involved in all of them (see pp. 90–91).

Taoist monks taught their disciples to hold their consciousness in the region of the navel, and through a deliberate process of visualization and

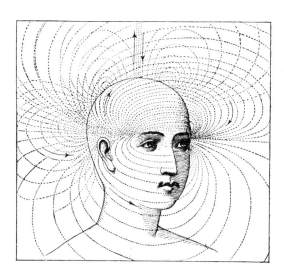

Force lines of the psycho-magnetic field surrounding the human head. According to Babbitt these curves of force can be thrown around people at a great distance in order to influence, attract or heal them. (Babbitt, 'Principles of Light and Colour'.)

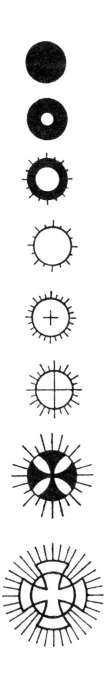

breathing exercises transfer the energies upward through the solar plexus to the head, thus stimulating the Golden Flower or lotus of the soul to bloom. The monks of the Orthodox Church in Russia and Greece have for centuries used the 'prayer of the heart', or 'Jesus Prayer' as it is commonly called. The technique consists of focusing the attention in the heart centre and repeating over and over, with deep concentration upon the words, 'Lord Jesus Christ, Son of God, have mercy on me.' It is a simple prayer that can be employed by anyone at any time in order to calm the mind and focus it in the heart of their being. Other schools of thought advise that the consciousness be focused in the head in the region of the crown or Ajna chakra. The placing of the consciousness in any special area is designed to bring about certain aspects of spiritual growth. For this reason meditation is best carried out under the supervision of a competent teacher, so that some of the very real dangers that lie along the inner path can be avoided.

The purpose of meditation is to purify the lower vehicles of manifestation and align them with the soul, thus providing a clear channel of expression for the purpose and energies of the spiritual source of power within. The surrendering of the lower to the higher is often marked by periods of deep inner crisis for the individual, but they lead on to expanded awareness. Dag Hammarskjöld must have experienced this when he wrote one night in his journal:

> But at some moment I did answer Yes to Someone – or Something – and from that hour I was certain that existence is meaningful and that, therefore, my life in self-surrender had a goal.

Vivekananda, at one stage during his meditation practices, reached a point in which everything he looked at appeared to be wreathed in flames, even the grains of rice in his bowl. His Master, Sri Ramakrishna, drew him out of this state of consciousness and explained that there was work for him to do in the world, and that he must return from this level of awareness or he would die within three weeks, consumed by the energies pouring through him. Nijinsky, the Russian dancer, without a spiritual guide, was less fortunate and ended his days writing repeatedly in his diary, 'God is fire in the head.' The path to enlightenment is no doubt beset with dangers (see p. 60); but it is equally a way of joy that culminates in the Inner Radiance being expressed through the subtle bodies of man. According to the Indian teachings these crisis points can lead to inner transformations which occur as a series of releases from the illusions of the worlds inhabited by the lower-self. It is clear that, whatever path the aspirant to wisdom treads, he must count the cost and know that much hard work and sacrifice will be required of him. T. S. Eliot sums it all up in the final lines of 'Little Gidding':

> A condition of complete simplicity
> (Costing nothing less than everything)
> And all shall be well and
> All manner of things shall be well
> When the tongues of flame are in-folded
> Into the crowned knot of fire
> And the fire and the rose are one.

These symbols often appear in the illustrations of haloes and are used to indicate the degree of spiritual awareness of the individual. From the top: dormant or latent principle; slightly awakened; partly awakened and glowing; awakened and glowing; first and second degrees of connection with the Christ; connection with the Logos. (Powell, 'The Causal Body'.)

Auras are often depicted as a field of flames surrounding the physical body, signifying that the individual has passed through the burning grounds of existence in the three worlds, and that all the dross has been burnt away to reveal the pure gold of the Spirit within. When the fires of the physical form have united with those of the soul and spirit the life of man blazes forth as an expression of Light. (Muhammad's vision of Gabriel on Mount Hira, illumination by Ahmed Nur Ibn Mustafa, from ms. *Life of the Prophet*, Turkey, 1368.)

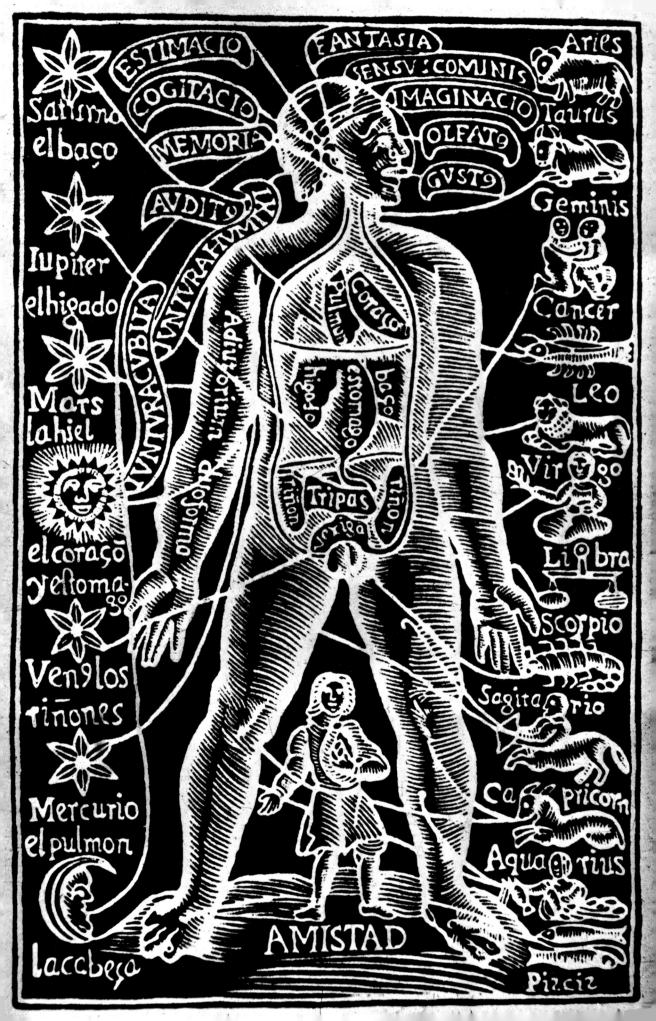

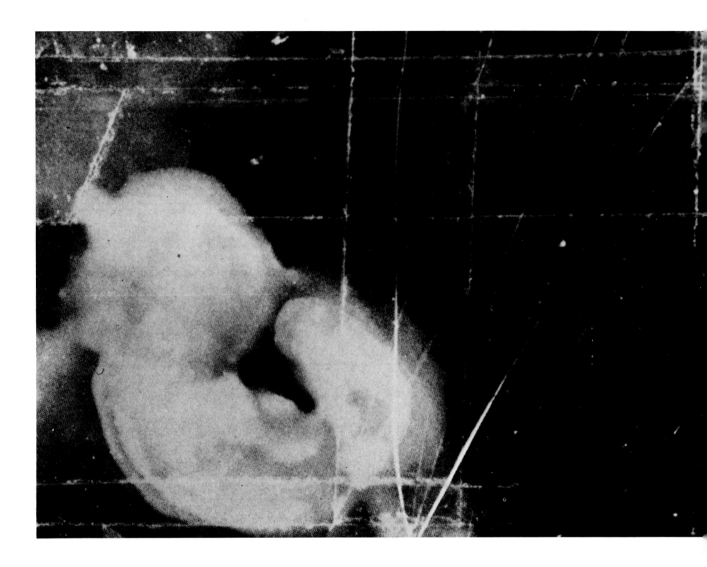

The ancient teachers believed that the zodiac with its twelve divisions formed the body of a vast being which they called the macrocosmic or heavenly man. This pattern, they claimed, reflected itself in microcosmic man, who came under the celestial influences that flowed in from the universe. The various organs of the human form, diseases and medicines were related to specific zodiacal signs. Paracelsus said: 'Medicine is in the will of the stars and is guided and directed by the stars. What belongs to the brain is directed to the brain by Luna; what belongs to the spleen is directed to the spleen by Saturn; what belongs to the heart is directed to the heart by Sol; and similarly to the kidneys by Venus, to the liver by Jupiter, to the bile by Mars.' Such factors played an important role in the traditional practice of healing. (Zodiacal man, woodcut, Spain, 15th–16th c.)

This radionic photograph taken in the 1950s shows a three-month foetus in the womb. Here the etheric body of the child silently absorbs the life-forces and cosmic patterns that will determine its qualities and characteristics for the coming incarnation. Perhaps the most remarkable aspect of this picture is the fact that it was obtained from the radiations of energy flowing from a blood spot donated by the mother, who was 54 miles from the camera when the exposure was made. In this process no light whatsoever touches the film, but the energy creating the image on the plate is so powerful that in places the emulsion is etched through to the glass. (Radionic photograph from blood spot of pregnant woman, De La Warr Laboratories, Oxford, England, 1950s.)

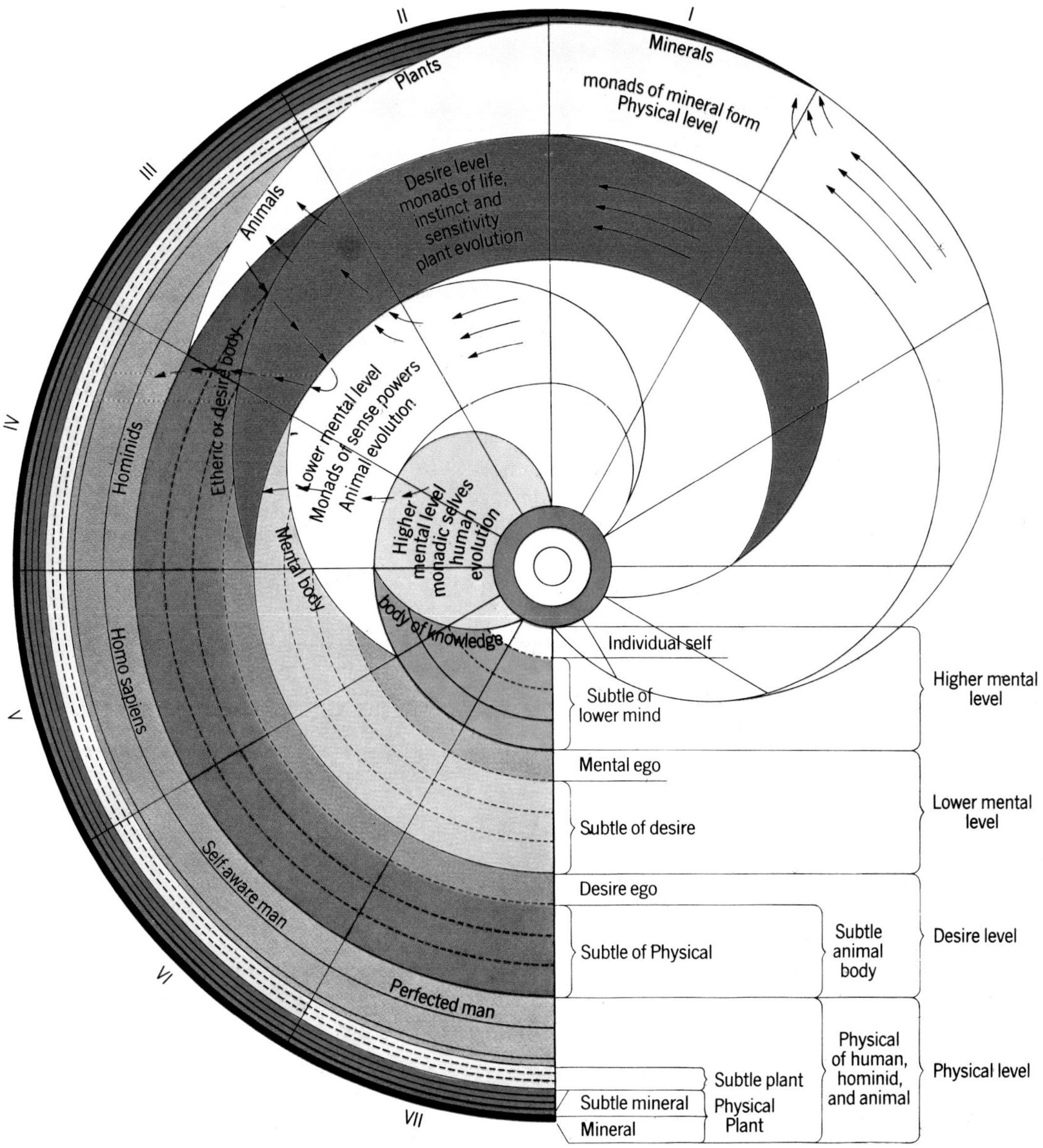
I
II
III
IV
V
VI
VII
Minerals
monads of mineral form
Physical level
Plants
Animals
Desire level
monads of life,
instinct and
sensitivity
plant evolution
Hominids
Etheric or desire body
Lower mental level
Monads of sense powers
Animal evolution
Higher mental level
monadic selves
human evolution
Mental body
body of knowledge
Homo sapiens
Self-aware man
Perfected man
Individual self
Subtle of
lower mind
Higher mental
level
Mental ego
Subtle of desire
Lower mental
level
Desire ego
Subtle of Physical
Subtle
animal
body
Desire level
Physical
of human,
hominid,
and animal
Physical level
Subtle plant
Subtle mineral
Physical
Plant
Mineral

The seven major spinal chakras (see pp. 27, 84) are here represented by symbols used in the Indian teachings. The crown chakra or Gate of Brahma is unfolded as a vast lotus filling the picture. The triangles of spirit and matter are blended to form a six-pointed star, as the yogi contemplates the Divine Reality. (The seven spinal chakras, painting by Mihran K. Serailian, USA, 1962.)

This chart depicts the various levels of the cosmic life that man lives within. The lowest and most physical aspect we are able to discern with our ordinary senses, but as the matter of each level becomes more attenuated the development of clairvoyance and finally intuition is required to observe the inner planes. The chart separates out each aspect of matter and illustrates it as a level; but in reality these planes interpenetrate each other to form a homogeneous field: the presence of the soul and spirit, Christ and God, are an immediate reality. No distance exists between the lower-self and the Reality. (Chart of the cosmic levels by Sri Madhara Ashish, India, 1970.)

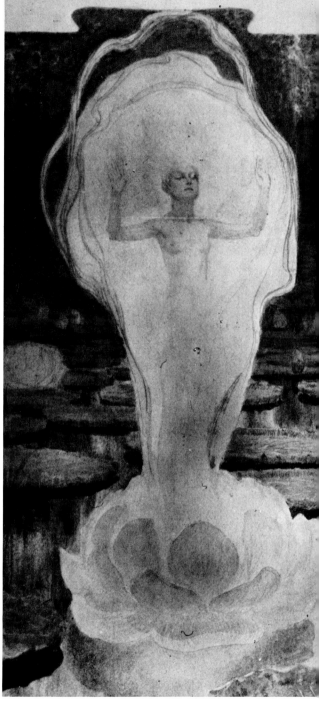

Life in its myriad forms depends on water for its existence. References in religious writings to rivers and water have a deep spiritual significance. St John (4:10) speaks of the living water which has the power to perfect the nature of man and make him whole. From the Christ flow the 'higher waters' of the Divine Life which re-generate and nourish man's under-standing of heavenly things. Rivers, like the Tree of Life, are the pathway along which the aspirant travels to the Godhead. The Nymph of the River Lo depicts this inner journey with flowing kimono and streaming ribbons symbolizing the energies of her aura. (Painting, China.)

The lotus has long been used to symbolize the inner nature of man, with his lower-self, rooted in the mud of the material world, rising through the waters of the astral or emotional nature into the air where the bloom of the soul unfolds in the fiery light of the spiritual sun. (The Soul of the Lotus, watercolour painting by Frank Kupka, Bohemia, 1898.)

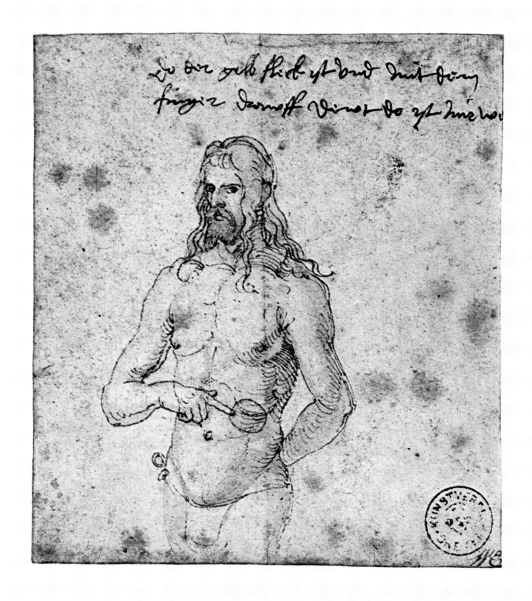

The spleen lies in the upper left part of the abdomen and serves as a reservoir for blood. The physical organ is simply the externalization of a subtle force centre which is directly responsible for absorbing the solar or pranic forces from the sun and distributing their vitalizing qualities to the physical form by way of the etheric body. In a letter believed to have been written by Albrecht Dürer to his physician, a sketch depicts the spleen as a sun-like disc, symbolizing the relationship of this organ to the forces flowing from that planet. William Blake portrays this same energizing force as a young, powerful and vibrant deity surrounded by a predominantly yellow auric field. (Self-portrait drawing by Albrecht Dürer, Germany, 16th c.; The Sun at his Eastern Gate, watercolour by William Blake, England, 19th c.)

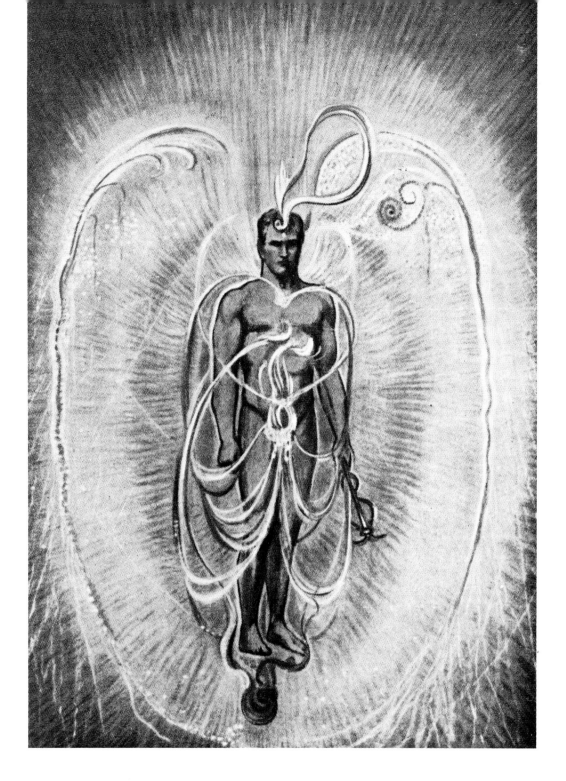

The mental body of man is a radiant field of energy currents, surrounding and interpenetrating the physical vehicle. Its heart-like shape is strikingly reminiscent of Babbitt's atom (see p. 19), with spiralling energy patterns flowing throughout. The energy current arising at the forehead has been called the magician's crest, which becomes more vital when the energies of the soul and the lower-self unite. It acts as a sensor, registering the activities of the other minds and thought currents that make their impress upon it. The mythical unicorn, with its single horn, symbolizes the unfolded spiritual nature of man. Chinese mandarins wore a peacock's feather to represent the magician's crest, and the Indians of North America the feather of the eagle. The hair style of Bear Bull, a Blackfoot, clearly illustrates this aspect of man's subtle anatomy. (The silver shield of the mental body, illustration by M. from *The Dayspring of Youth*, 1970; Bear Bull, photograph by Edward S. Curtis, USA, 1926.)

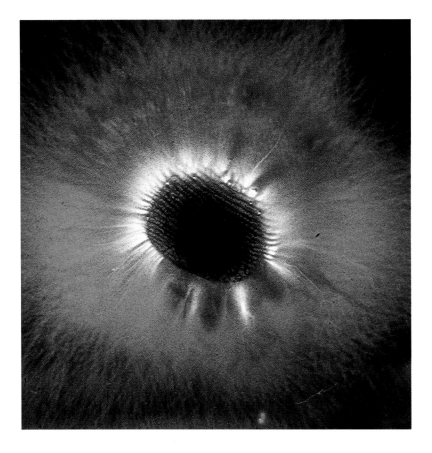

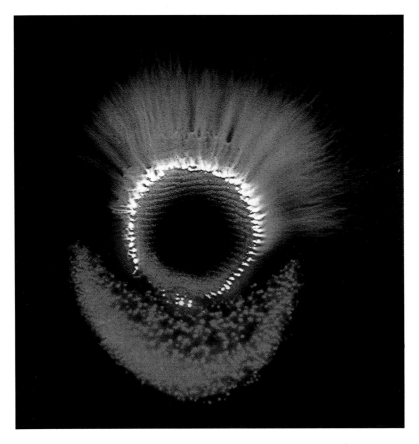

The quality of an individual's aura permeates the place where that person lives, providing a record of states of health, character and spiritual attainment. These factors can be identified by those sensitive enough to register them; Edgar Cayce, the seer of Virginia Beach, frequently made diagnostic readings, for those who sought his help, from the impressions they left in their environment. Yves Klein sought to express these intangible fields and impressions in his paintings, even going so far as to put on an exhibition of empty rooms in which he had created 'atmospheres'. Kirlian or high voltage photography, begun more than thirty years ago in Russia by Semyon Kirlian, shows the energy emission around various objects. Both Soviet and American researchers feel that information about a person's physical, emotional and mental condition can be drawn from these pictures. The discovery of a physical explanation for the Kirlian phenomena would in no way rule out the possibility that the image appearing on the film is an aspect of the aura. (Kirlian photographs of finger, showing a state of meditation and the red of anger, by Daniel A. Keintz; The Vampire, painting by Yves Klein, France, 1960.)

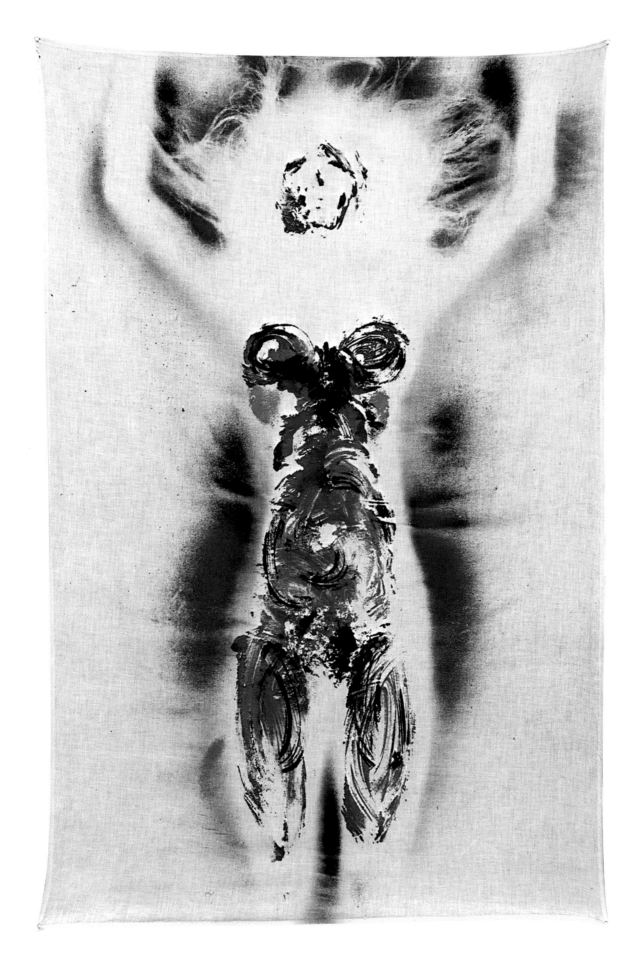

In Tantric tradition the conduits of vital force or *prana* are called nadis. They form an intricate web of subtle energy fibres that permeate the physical form. Certain texts speak of 350,000 nadis, through which the solar and lunar energies flow like the patterns of ocean currents. Of these fourteen are major nadis; the Ida, Pingala and Sushumna being the three principle ones. They are also known as Ganga (Ida), Yamuna (Pingala) and Sarasvati (Sushumna), after the three sacred rivers of India. Along the Sushumna, which is considered the most important nadis of all, lie the chakras, which act as the main receptors and distributors of energy to the subtle bodies. The negative lunar current of the Ida begins at the base and to the left of the Sushumna. It has been described as pale in colour and cooling in its action. The positive solar current of the Pingala begins at the right, having a heating action and being ruddy in colour. These two nadis are said to cross the Sushumna or etheric spinal cord from side to side, meeting at the Ajna chakra to form the figure of the Caduceus. Along these pathways the experienced yogi leads the inner serpent power of Kundalini, in a controlled and precise geometric pattern, from the base of the spine to the head. (The nadis, diagram, Tibet.)

Tao adepts taught that to become alive and immortal man must learn to be one with the Primal Force. This force was described as Light, which, if concentrated upon and circulated in a correct manner through the subtle anatomy, brought all the powers of the body or lower-self before the throne of the Heavenly Heart in the forehead. This culminated in the prolongation of life, the uniting of the forces of the sun and the moon, and the creation of an immortal body. The centres through which the Light circulates in this system correspond in many ways to those of Tantric philosophy; they are referred to as a sevenfold row of 'trees' or body openings, and symbolized by human or animal figures. (The circulation of the body, after a tablet in the Monastery of the White Clouds, near Peking, China.)

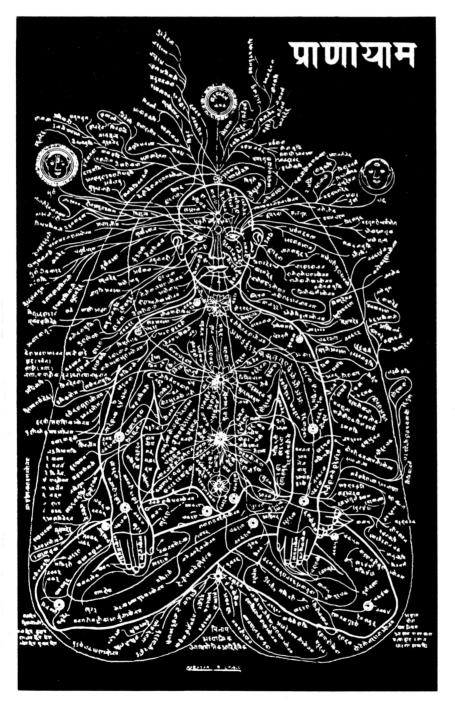

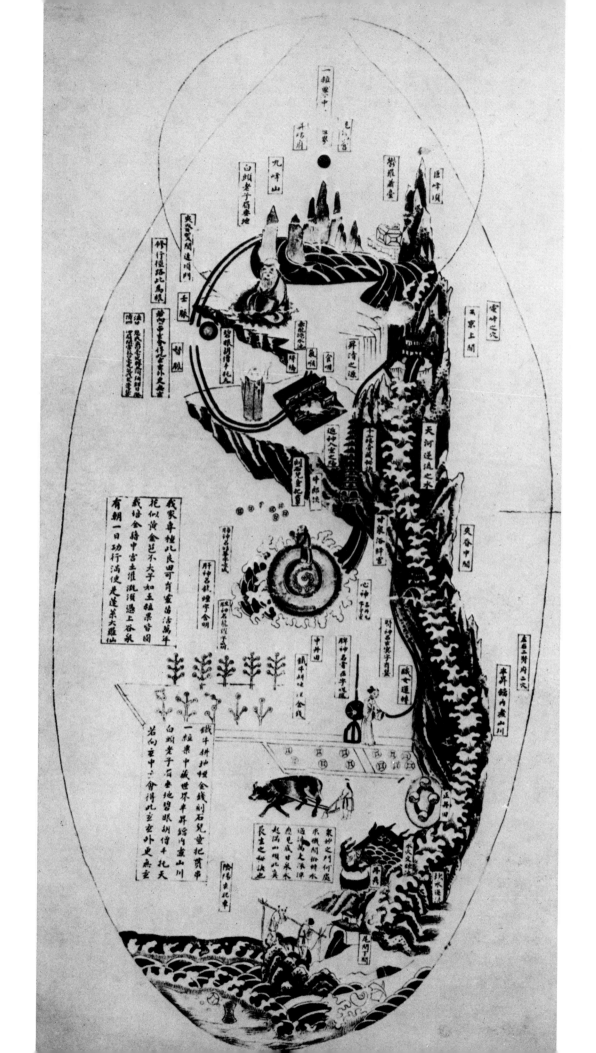

Purification of the lower-self is a theme common to all true religious practice. Careful control of the mind and emotions, and a natural diet, aid in harmonizing the forces of the three bodies that the soul uses as vehicles of manifestation. Mary the mother of Jesus, through long preparation and discipline as an Essene initiate, had so purified her nature that she could provide for her child a physical body of such perfection that it was capable of becoming a vehicle for the Christ. (Madonna, detail of the Concert of Angels, painting by Grünewald, Germany, early 16th c.)

The three 'vestures' or bodies of the Buddha are called the Dharmakaya, the Sambhogakaya and the Nirmanakaya. These vehicles are of such purity and magnetic power, arising as they do directly from the Monad, that a Buddha can manifest simultaneously in the three worlds: in this world as a Master of the Wisdom; on His own plane as a Bodhisattva; and as a Dhyani Buddha on a yet higher plane. Yet the Three are but One, even if the work He does seems to be the work of three separate Existences. So great is the power of a Buddha's vestures that Tibetans believe that to be in physical incarnation at the same time as a Buddha will greatly hasten their own spiritual evolution. (Shaka, painting on silk, Japan, 12th c.)

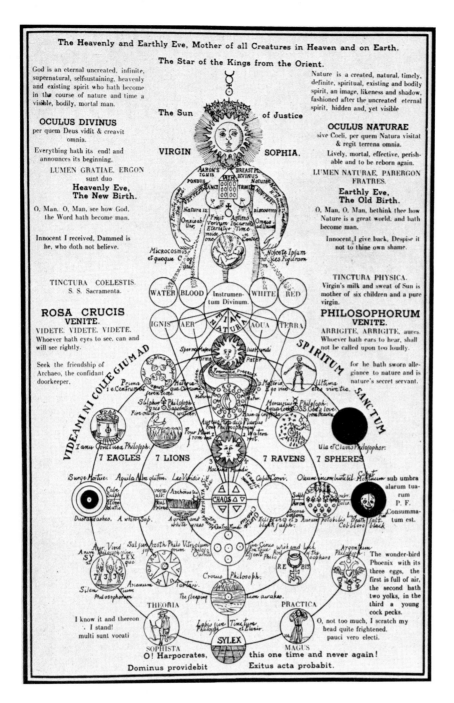

The Heavenly and Earthly Eve, Mother of all Creatures in Heaven and on Earth.

The Star of the Kings from the Orient.

God is an eternal uncreated, infinite, supernatural, selfsustaining, heavenly and existing spirit who hath become in the course of nature and time a visible, bodily, mortal man.

OCULUS DIVINUS
per quem Deus vidit & creavit omnia.

Everything hath its end! and announces its beginning.

LUMEN GRATIAE, ERGON
sunt duo
**Heavenly Eve,
The New Birth.**

O, Man, O, Man, see how God, the Word hath become man.

Innocent I received, Dammed is he, who doth not believe.

TINCTURA COELESTIS.
S. S. Sacramenta.

**ROSA CRUCIS
VENITE.**
VIDETE. VIDETE. VIDETE.
Whoever hath eyes to see, can and will see rightly.

Seek the friendship of Archaeo, the confidant doorkeeper.

The Sun   of Justice

VIRGIN   SOPHIA.

Nature is a created, natural, timely, definite, spiritual, existing and bodily spirit, an image, likeness and shadow, fashioned after the uncreated eternal spirit, hidden and, yet visible

OCULUS NATURAE
sive Coeli, per quem Natura visitat & regit terrena omnia.

Lively, mortal, effective, perishable and to be reborn again.

LUMEN NATURAE, PARERGON
FRATRES.
**Earthly Eve,
The Old Birth.**

O, Man, O, Man, bethink thee how Nature is a great world, and hath become man.

Innocent I give back. Despise it not to thine own shame.

TINCTURA PHYSICA.
Virgin's milk and sweat of Sun is mother of six children and a pure virgin.

**PHILOSOPHORUM
VENITE.**
ARRIGITE, ARRIGITE, aures. Whoever hath ears to hear, shall not be called upon too loudly.

for he hath sworn allegiance to nature and is nature's secret servant.

7 EAGLES   7 LIONS   7 RAVENS   7 SPHERES

THEORIA   PRACTICA

I know it and thereon ∴ I stand! multi sunt vocati

The wonder-bird Phoenix with its three eggs, the first is full of air, the second hath two yolks, in the third a young cock pecks.

O, not too much, I scratch my head quite frightened. pauci vero electi.

SOPHISTA   SYLEX   MAGUS
O! Harpocrates,   this one time and never again!
Dominus providebit.   Exitus acta probabit.

Eve stands representative of the material aspect of creation, the matrix from which a multitude of forms emerge. The Divine act of creating Eve from the side of Adam divides the One; and the positive and negative or masculine and feminine polarities arise. Their interaction as spirit and matter, or Yin and Yang, produces the life forms of all beings. The feminine aspect of creation plays an important role in the beliefs and teachings of many peoples and is a dominant theme amongst the *sangoma* (witchdoctors) of Southern Africa. This female *sangoma* wears the symbol of the Earth Spirit, a beaded diamond shape at her throat. On her head is a wig of beads, representing the flow of the spirit from above. In many instances wigs treated with haematite are worn for ritual purposes because this mineral is revered as the blood of the mother earth. (The Heavenly and Earthly Eve, from *A Christian Rosenkreuz Anthology*; Ghatebi, a female *sangoma*, photograph by Pierre Hinch, South Africa, 1970s.)

The Sahasrara, the crown chakra or thousand-petalled lotus, is located in the successive subtle bodies just above the top of the head. It is known as the throne of spiritual dominion and here, according to Indian tradition, Shiva the destroyer of ignorance and illusion dwells. When fully awakened it draws the feminine aspect or matter up into heaven to be transformed into spiritual substance. The Assumption of the Virgin Mary, in Christian tradition, symbolizes this profoundly important spiritual event, which heralds the point in evolution at which the need for physical incarnation no longer exists. St John wrote of this, 'He goeth out no more.' In Buddhist teachings this point of development is symbolized by the Bodhisattva, who then turns back towards the world of men and vows to return until all sentient beings have reached perfection. (The crown chakra, illustration by C. W. Leadbeater from *The Chakras*; Assumption of the Virgin, detail of painting by Girolamo da Vincenza, Italy, 15th c.)

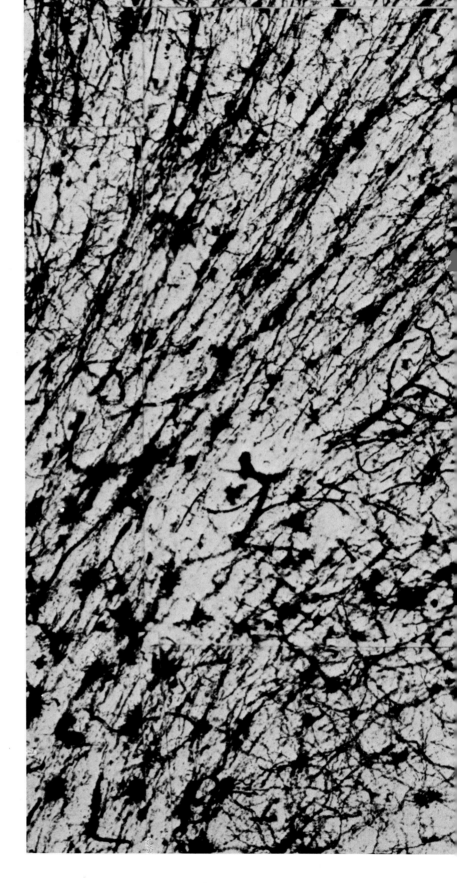

High-magnification pictures of neurones in the cortex of the cerebellum, which deals with the control of movement, reveal a web-like structural pattern that may well be a reflection of the nadis or etheric nervous system that the Vedic seers described in their writings several thousand years ago. The artist Jackson Pollock seems to have captured this pattern through the intuitive and spontaneous application of paint to canvas, wherein the intellect, held in abeyance, allowed the synchronistic out-flowing pattern of an inner reality to come directly into expression. (Neurones in the cerebellar cortex, photograph taken by the Golgi method, from D. A. Scholl, *Organization of the Cerebral Cortex*, London 1956; Europe 1950, detail of painting by Jackson Pollock, USA, 1950.)

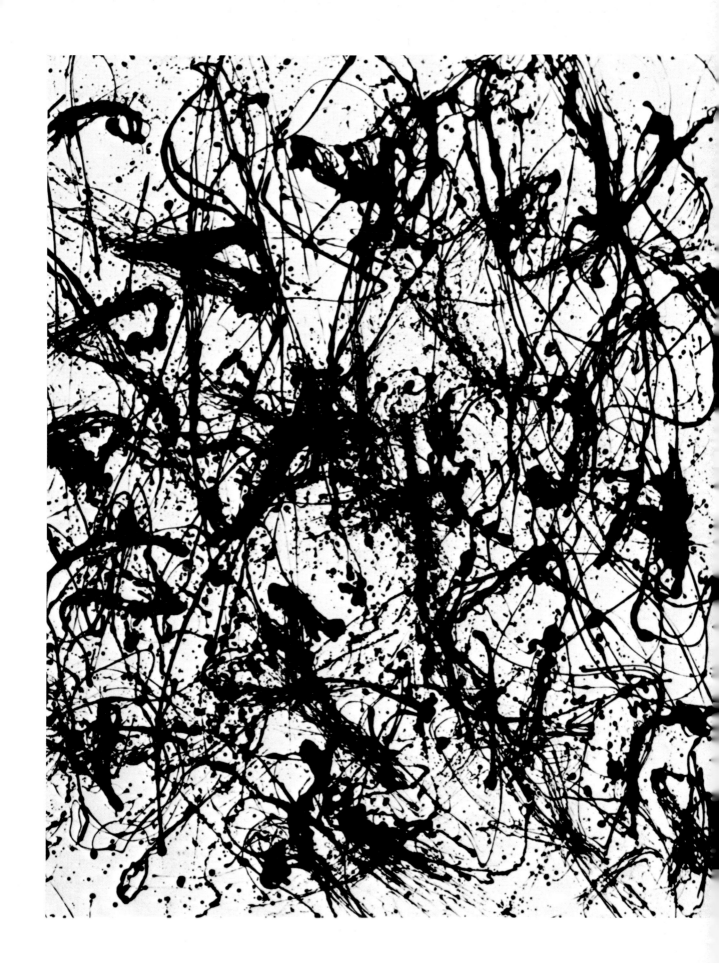

The head of Minerva represents wisdom, and shows the dynamic energy fields of the pineal and pituitary glands blending to form the third or spiritual eye. When these fields blend harmoniously, and the forces of the higher and lower natures are coordinated, the corona or halo appears around the head. The tail of the sacred asp touching the medulla draws the fires or energies of the spine into the pituitary body and upwards into the pineal gland. This keeps the psychic forces, which pour through the individual, sublimated to the higher chakras. (Head of Minerva, painting by Mihran K. Serailian, USA, 1962.)

The pineal gland, according to many philosophers, is the seat of the soul, acting as a link between the visible and invisible worlds. Descartes is often quoted as saying, 'In man, soul and body touch each other only at a single point, the pineal gland in the head.' Activation of the brain cells in the region of the pineal through prayer and meditation is said to bring about an awakening of intuitive perception. This gland has often been likened to an alchemical retort, which releases its spiritual essence into man when the dross has been burnt from his personality; its action transforms him into a bearer of Light. (The pineal gland, photograph by Lennart Nilsson, 1974.)

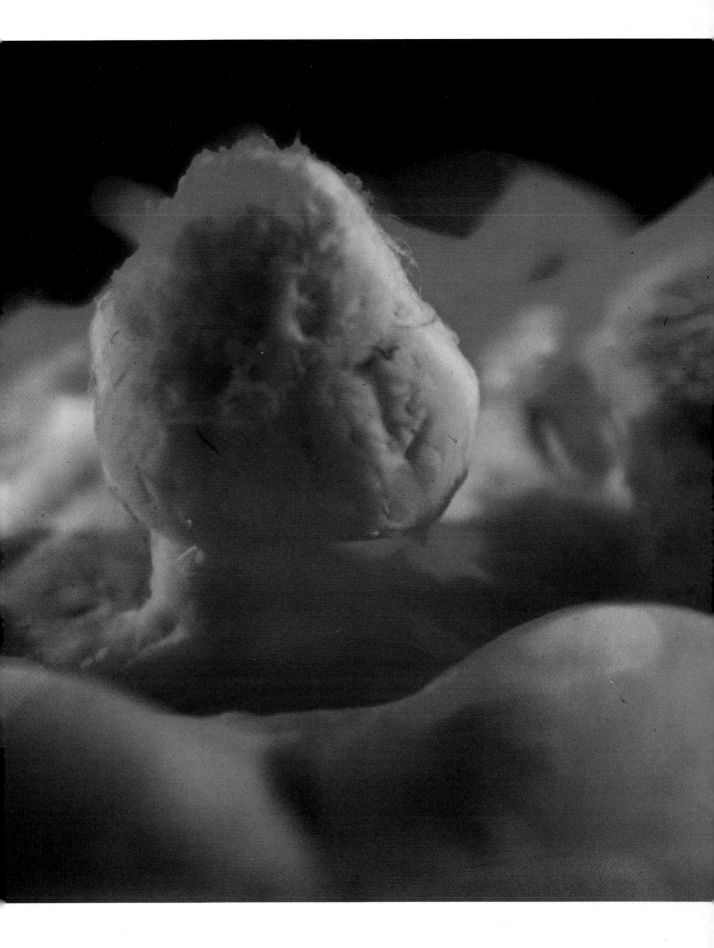

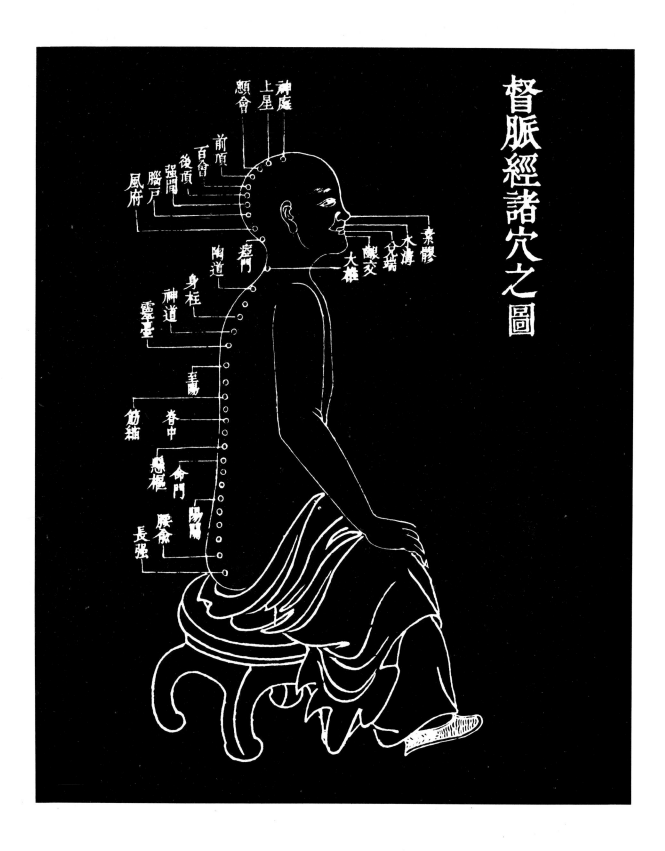

督脈經諸穴之圖

神庭
上星
顖會
前頂
百會
後頂
強間
腦戶
風府
瘂門
陶道
身柱
神道
靈臺
至陽
筋縮
脊中
懸樞
命門
陽關
腰俞
長強

素髎
水溝
兌端
齦交
大椎

Ling-shu, an ancient Chinese medical text, contains twelve diagrams of man's inner force centres. The entire system, known as the grand circulation, is here divided into two courses. The descending or involuntary circulation runs from the lower lip, through the chest and abdomen to the tip of the spine. The rising or controlled circulation runs from the tip of the spine, along the spine itself and over the top of the head to the

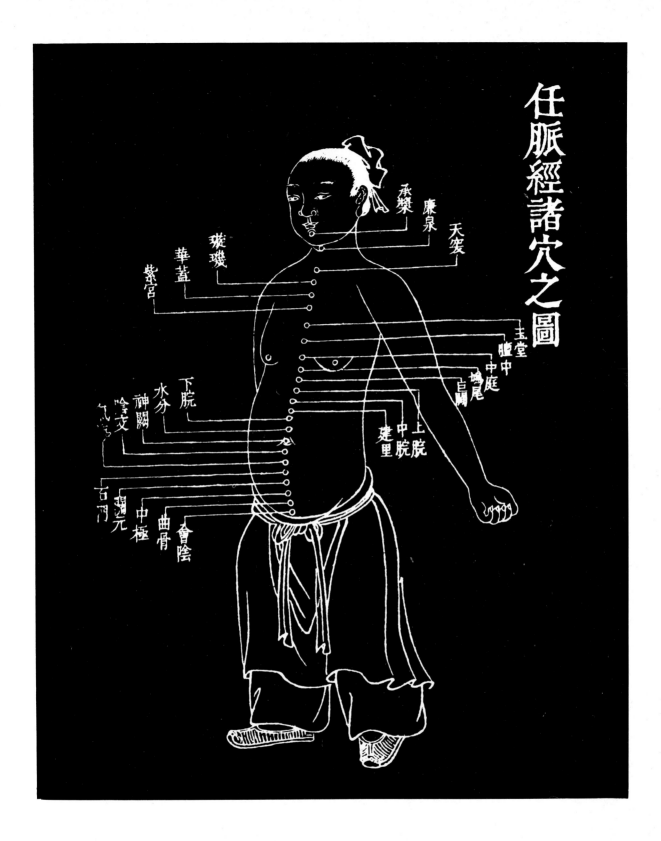

任脈經諸穴之圖

承漿　廉泉　天突
璇璣
華蓋
紫宮
玉堂
膻中
中庭
鳩尾
巨闕
下脘
水分
神闕
陰交
氣海
中脘　上脘
建里
石門
關元
中極
曲骨
會陰

upper lip. The Taoist yogis coupled deep, rhythmic breathing with visualization techniques to circulate psychic energies through this system of force centres, thus harmonizing the polarities of Yin and Yang to awaken cosmic consciousness and bring about total identification with the macrocosm. (Centres on controlled and involuntary courses, from Chang Chung-Yuan, *Creativity and Taoism.*)

Birds frequently symbolize spiritual elevation, and their wings are added to men as symbols of their capacity to transcend the limitations of the physical realms and to act as intermediaries bringing messages and visions from God. The soul is said to have 'the wings of an eagle', linking the worlds of spirit and form; and he who would fly upward must be pure. Icarus symbolizes the uninitiated, unregenerate man who forces his way into the presence of higher spiritual energies without correct preparation. Their power flowing through his unpurified nature meets such resistance that it burns and destroys all that it contacts. Anyone who deliberately sets out to raise the Kundalini is especially prone to such danger, for if he succeeds in some measure in attaining this goal, he may well disrupt his nervous system, resulting in pathological changes of a physical and psychological nature. At worst, according to Blavatsky, the power unleashed through his form can burn the 'seed atoms' of his bodies and he becomes a 'lost soul' incapable of reincarnating for aeons. (The Fall of Icarus, detail of painting by Joos de Momper the Younger, Netherlands, 16th–17th c.)

The pagan emblem of the dove appears in Christianity representing the third person of the Holy Trinity, the builder of form, gentle, devout and pure. In the Annunciation the form-creating energies stream from God to be focused through the dove before entering the Virgin's head in the region of the pituitary gland, symbol of the form. The room in which the Virgin kneels may also be seen to represent the head, while she symbolizes the pituitary. Above her the peacock representing the pineal stands for wisdom and immortality. In the courtyard the Archangel Gabriel wears the emblems of both the Sahasrara and Ajna chakras upon his head. (Annunciation, by Carlo Crivelli, Italy, 15th c.)

LIBERTAS · ECCLESIASTICA

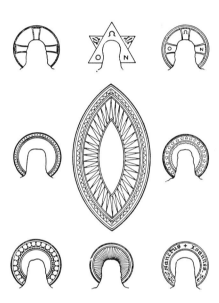

Haloes surrounding the heads of religious figures symbolize the radiations of inner light flowing outwards through the purified and consecrated personality. Straight, radiating lines in the halo represent the power of the sun or soul; curved lines indicate the lunar forces of the lower nature. Combinations of these lines are seen to represent a balance between the forces of the soul and personality. Here, in the Agony in the Garden, Christ's halo bears the cross within it, showing His direct and unobstructed contact with God. (Diagram of haloes by Manly Palmer Hall, from *Man, Grand Symbol of the Mysteries*; Christ at the Mount of Olives, detail of mosaic, St Mark's, Venice, 13th c.)

The physical, etheric, astral and mental bodies of man are mortal, and exist for a period of one incarnation only. The causal body, on the other hand, is relatively immortal as it persists until the initiation of the Crucifixion whereat man passes on to the way of higher evolution. The sacrifice of Christ's perfected lower nature upon the cross was followed, we are told, by darkness and silence for three hours. Then came the total renunciation of His very being as He placed His soul upon the altar of sacrifice. So devastating was this experience, as the power of the Spirit shattered His causal body, that the cry of questioning protest was torn from His lips, 'My God, my God, why hast Thou forsaken me?' There later followed the words, 'It is finished', as the magnitude of His accomplishment flooded His consciousness. Spirit and matter were now one; and He had demonstrated, for man as an individual and humanity as a whole, the Way that led to this union of perfection. (The Christ of St John of the Cross, painting by Salvador Dali, Spain, 1951.)

Themes

So closely can the mystic become identified with the Crucifixion, the initiation of Jesus Christ, that the stigmata will appear on his body and blood will flow from the wounds. Perhaps the best known example of this is the stigmatization of St Francis. In this century Padre Pio, an Italian monk, bore the stigmata; and although the Church placed him in an isolated monastery, many people sought the blessing of this beautiful soul. There are a number of instances on record where he displayed the capacity for bilocation, living in Italy but simultaneously appearing in England to administer healing to certain people.

The aura in medicine

Orthodox medicine does not recognize the existence of the human aura; but a number of medical doctors have investigated this aspect of man. One of the first to do so was Dr Walter Kilner, head of the electro-therapy department at St Thomas's Hospital in London. He was familiar with the Theosophical literature pertaining to the aura and etheric double. In 1908 he began experimenting with dicyanin screens in order to make the human aura visible. The dye used in the screens had a definite effect upon the human eye, making it sensitive to radiations not normally registered, and through this method Kilner could see the auric field around his patients. In 1911 he published his findings in a book called *The Human Atmosphere* which came complete with diagrams and screens. Kilner claimed that the aura had distinct inner and outer components, and that they showed changes when disease was present. None of Kilner's work showed any indication that he could see the chakras; perhaps he could visualize only the coarsest aspects of the aura through the screens. He was adamant that the phenomena observed were physical in nature and in no way occult. In recent years Dr John Pierrakos, director of the Institute for Bioenergetic Analysis in New York, has observed the aura directly without the use of screens. His findings bear a close resemblance to those of Kilner, and he too has attempted to apply these observations for diagnostic purposes in his own practice. Another outstanding physician, Dr Shafica Karagulla, works with sensitives, clairvoyants who can see the auric fields as well as the various bodies of man and the chakras. Their descriptions of the alterations taking place in the chakras and the subtle bodies have been found to have an accurate and direct relationship to the actual physical diseases recorded in the patients' medical case-histories. In many instances the sensitives can detect pathological changes in the aura before they make a physical appearance. No doubt the day will come when science will devise instrumentation that can scan the human aura and make visible these subtle fields.

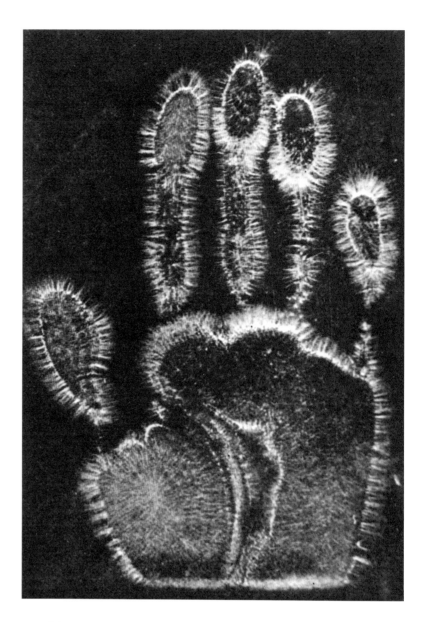

One of the earliest examples of electro-photography, showing the radiating lines of energy from a human hand, taken in the late nineteenth century. The energy lines radiating at right angles from the surfaces of the hand fit descriptions given by clairvoyants of the etheric body. (Photograph by Baraduc, from Milner and Smart.)

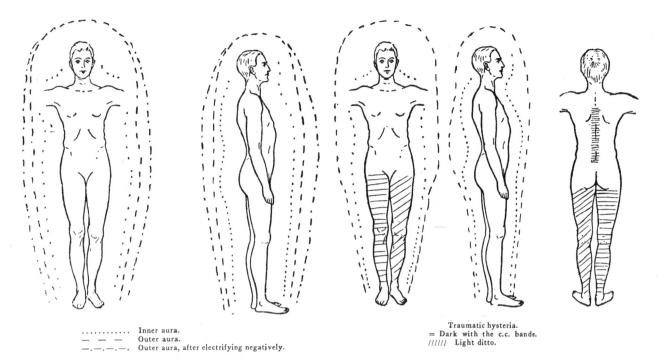

.... Inner aura.
— — — Outer aura.
—.—.—.— Outer aura, after electrifying negatively.

Traumatic hysteria.
= Dark with the c.c. bands.
/////// Light ditto.

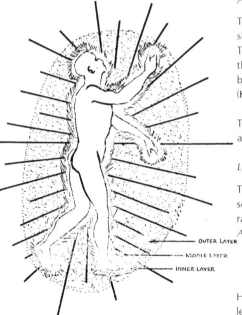

OUTER LAYER
MIDDLE LAYER
INNER LAYER

Above, left to right:

The human aura according to Kilner, showing an inner and outer component. The third and outer tracing represents the outer component after the aura has been subjected to an electrical charge. (Kilner, *The Aura.*)

The aura in traumatic hysteria showing alterations to the field. (Kilner, *The Aura.*)

Left:

The three layers of the human aura as seen and described by Dr John C. Pierrakos. (Regush, *Exploring the Human Aura.*)

Hypothetical transverse sections of epileptic auras. (Kilner, *The Aura.*)

Below:

Some of the energy lines detected by Dutch radiesthetist Dr Phillipi in his own aura at the level of the abdomen. This tracing was done by placing a sheet of paper on a board and then using a pendulum to detect nodal points in the force field. Each point is then joined to form the outlines of the field. Drawn in the early 1960s, it shows outward flowing lines of force that tally with descriptions given by Castaneda and Karagulla of the tentacle-like projections that occur in the solar plexus area. Sensitives working with Dr Karagulla have observed that some people have the capacity to drain others of energy by applying these tentacle-like structures to their auras. My own observations indicate that individuals suffering from post-traumatic neurosis are peculiarly adept at this.

Transverse sections

Males

Females

Fig. g

Fig. h

Fig. i

Fig. k

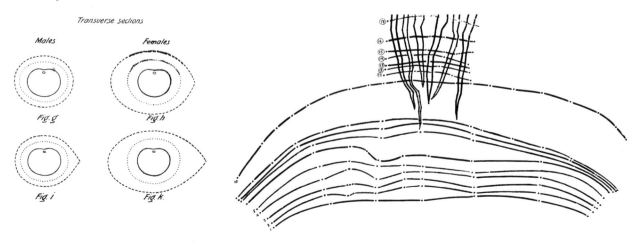

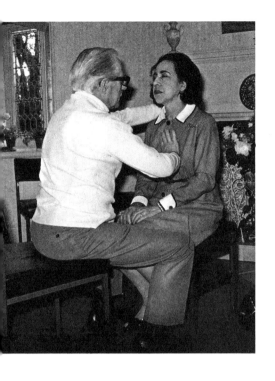

Healing by hand

The healing arts over the years have been broadly divided into two categories: those which are strictly physical in their approach to the problems of health and disease, and those which are spiritually oriented and take the concept of total man into consideration. Until relatively recent times the orthodox body of medicine has had no time for spiritual healing, and in many cases the spiritual healer has had little time for his orthodox counterpart. Today however the more enlightened and perceptive practitioners of both sides see the need to work in harmony and cooperate in their efforts to heal the patient, often with outstanding results. The ideal healer, it would seem, is one who has qualifications in a recognized healing art plus the knowledge and capacity to function as a spiritual healer. Aldous Huxley, in a typically prophetic vein, referred to this type of individual when he wrote of the 'neuro-theologist', who would think of people simultaneously in terms of the Clear Light of the Void and the vegetative nervous system; in other words in terms of the totality of their spiritual and subtle bodies and their physical form.

This page:

Healing has been defined as the restoration of harmony to the complexity of energies that make up the bodies of man. The hands, each with a minor chakra in the central area of the palm, have been used since time immemorial to direct healing energies through the ailing patient. Here Gilbert Anderson treats a patient for emphysema.

Internationally known healer Harry Edwards claims to work with spirit guides and discarnate healers on the inner planes during his healing sessions.

Franz Anton Mesmer developed the concept of animal magnetism, a fluid-like energy that surrounded and permeated all forms. The human body, he claimed, had poles and other properties analogous to magnets, and through this magnetic medium one body could act upon another to bring about healing. Despite, or perhaps because of, the many remarkable cures effected by this method at his Paris clinic, a Royal Commission that had been set up in 1784 to investigate his claims predictably reported: 'The imagination does everything, the magnetism nothing.' (Projecting Magnetism, from E. Sibley, *A Key to Magic and the Occult Sciences*, c. 1800.)

Massage and the finger pressure techniques of Shiatsu are designed to release and normalize the flow of energies through the organism. (Jacques de Langre, *Do-in*, Oakland, Calif., 1971.)

The chart shows some of the Shiatsu trigger points to which pressure is applied. One advantage of this system of balancing energies is that the individual can treat himself. (Tokujiro Namikoshi, *Shiatsu*, Hackensack, N.J., 1969.)

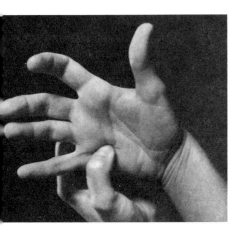

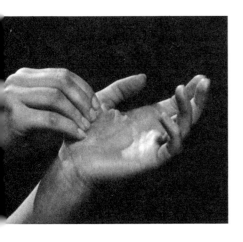

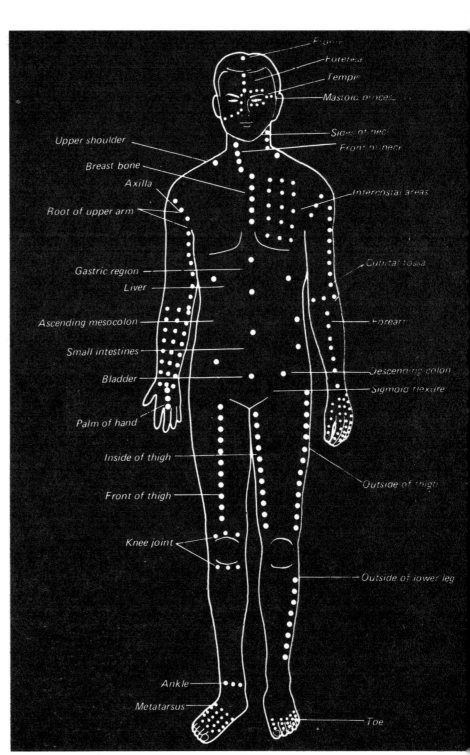

Acupuncture

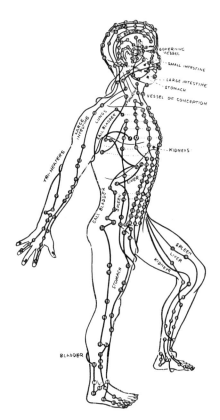

Acupuncture has been one of the traditional forms of healing in China for many thousands of years. It is based on the theory that all illness arises from imbalances in the flow of energies through pathways in the human body called meridians. Acupuncturists sedate or stimulate these energy flows by placing fine needles in the body at certain points and thus restore health. Tradition has it that almost five thousand years ago the Yellow Emperor said to his physicians: 'I desire that all remedies apart from acupuncture be suppressed. I command that this method and knowledge shall be recorded and transmitted to future generations and that its laws shall be recorded, so that it will be easy to practise it and difficult to forget it.' The ensuing years led to treatises being written on the subject and the production of drawings showing the acupuncture points. Bronze statues of the human figure complete with holes to mark these points were cast, to be used in practical training and for examination purposes. Today acupuncture is increasingly being used in the western world, and physicians who once thought of disease in terms of organic pathology only, now view it in terms of energy flow and distribution.

Left:

Modern drawings showing meridians and acupuncture points. (Wu Wei P'ing, *Acupuncture*, 1962.)

Below:

Traditional drawing from China, Ming period, illustrating meridian and acupuncture points.

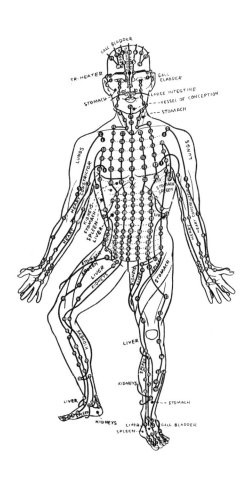

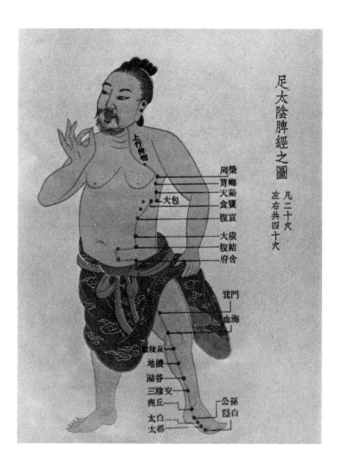

足太陰脾經之圖

凡二十穴
左右共四十穴

Traditional acupuncture needles are made of fine steel with a haft of copper wire wound around the shaft. In some instances needles of gold or silver are preferred for purposes of stimulation or sedation. The needle is inserted into the appropriate acupuncture point to the indicated depth, where it may be manipulated by the practitioner or simply left until, in response to a gentle pull, the flesh releases it easily. In China a needle placed at a certain point in the arm is frequently used to induce anaesthesia. It does of course require very skilful manipulation of the needle to bring this state about, but so effective is it that patients can undergo major surgery while fully conscious and without suffering any of the bad after-effects usually associated with western methods. (Acupuncture treatment, Hungary.)

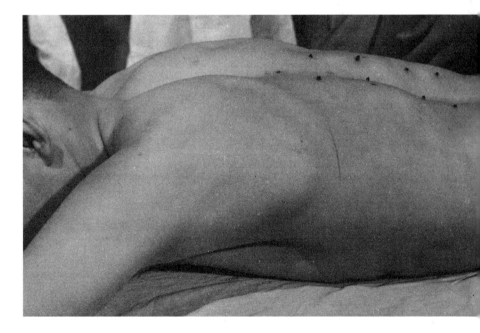

Moxa treatment of acupuncture points is most effectively done by burning a cone of artemisia at the selected point or points. In the west some practitioners use a moxa hammer which has a rounded head on one side and a pointed one on the other. This is heated over a spirit stove for a few seconds before applying to the point to be treated. The rounded head is used for sedation purposes and the pointed for stimulation.

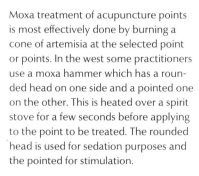

Etheric formative forces

Chang Tsai (1020–77) wrote: 'The Great Void cannot but consist of ether; this ether cannot but condense to form all things; and these things cannot but become dispersed so as to form once more the Great Void.' This ether or matter-energy was called Ch'i, or material cause. Later philosophers added to this the metaphysical principle referred to as Li, and Chu Hsi said: 'The creation of man depends simply upon the union of the principle with the ether. Heavenly principle, or T'ien Li, is surely vast and inexhaustible. All men's capacity to speak, move, think, and act, is entirely derived from the ether; and yet this ether principle inheres within.'

The Vedic seers of India held a similar opinion, saying that the world had its origin in ether . . . 'For all these beings take their rise from the ether only, and return into the ether. Ether is greater than these, ether is their rest.'

Underlying the dense, liquid and gaseous aspects of the physical body are four levels of attenuated matter known as the etheric. Rudolf Steiner called these the etheric formative forces, and identified them as the matrix upon which all physical forms are built. Each of these ethers is a constituent part of the etheric body of man, and they serve to connect his physical vehicle to the astral levels of his being. The first level is the warmth ether, related to electrical phenomena. The second is the light ether, wherein the quality of light is expressed. The third or chemical ether is the ether of sound and numbers, and the fourth or life ether is related to colour. Each one of these ethers gives rise to particular geometric forms. Where there is a predominance of warmth ether, spherical forms appear. The light ether gives rise to triangular forms, the chemical ether to discs or half-moon shapes. In the human body one can see the predominance of the light ether in the triangular form of the right adrenal gland, and the chemical ether in the half-moon shape of the left adrenal. The valves of the heart clearly show the formative forces of the chemical ether at work. The life ether tends to produce square forms. When these forces are in a state of harmony and free flow, the organism experiences health; if for any reason imbalances occur in these ethers, then the distortion or blockage creates changes in the physical body, and disease makes its appearance, precipitated as it were from the subtle to the physical level.

Left:

The sharp bright discs of the chemical ether. (All four photographs from Milner and Smart, *The Loom of Creation*.)

The life ether is apparently difficult to photograph, but its squaring off effect can be seen around the dark mass. Discs of the chemical ether also make their appearance in this picture.

Right:

The sparkling, striking out, triangular shapes of the light ether dominate this picture.

Clusters of highly evolved warmth ether spheres, reminiscent of electron microscope pictures of cells.
 These photographs represent the four etheric formative forces in their pristine state before they have been utilized to build forms.

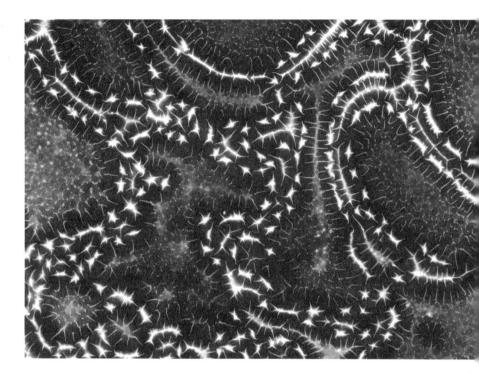

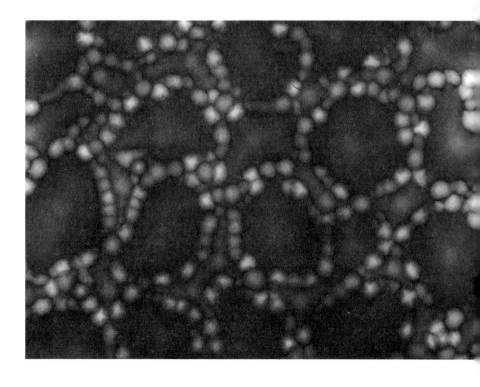

The aura in art

From earliest times man has attempted to depict the radiance and beauty of the human aura, and naturally it has fallen to the lot of the artist and visionary to carry out this most difficult and frustrating task. For the artist who has the benefit of a true inner sight to work from, the bewildering and often kaleidoscopic changes in colour and form of the aura are clearly impossible to capture on canvas. Early Buddhist and Christian painters and other visionaries right up to Blake circumvented this problem by stylizing the auric fields. Odilon Redon shows the aura as a diaphanous, pastel surround, its irregular shape giving the impression of a pulsating, moving field of energy.

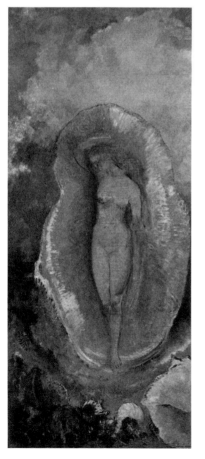

From left:

Navajo rock-painting of a mysterious angelic figure, New Mexico, early 18th c.

Buddhist sculpture with a series of lotus leaves and blossoms depicting the aura. (Wooden Kan-non, Nara, Japan, 9th c.)

The Birth of Venus, painting by Odilon Redon, 1912. (Kimbell Art Foundation, Fort Worth, Texas.)

Albion rose from where he labour'd, engraving by William Blake, 1780. (National Gallery of Art, Washington, D C.)

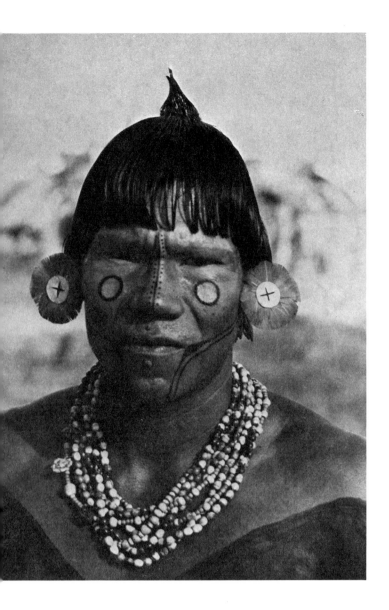

Adornment of the head

In all cultures the head has been adorned in a variety of ways in order to depict certain inner spiritual realities, and to draw the attention of others to this repository of power. Feathers, beads, paint and a variety of objects are arranged in such a manner as to represent the centres of force on the forehead and crown, or to symbolize the aura around the head itself. The chiefs or priests who were men of knowledge had the most distinctive form of adornment in keeping with their rank and spiritual understanding. The eyes, of course, often spoken of as the mirror of the soul, are potent manipulators of energy, and today as in the past, they are decorated in order to emphasize their presence.

Above:

A Karajá Indian in full ceremonial make-up with circular tribal marks on his cheeks and lower lip. Curiously, the circles on his cheeks and the circular feather decorations at each ear are located exactly where Tibetan sources place four of the minor chakras in the head. His hair is fashioned into an antenna-like peak in the area of the crown chakra and is reminiscent of portrayals of this force centre in Buddhist art.

A cowrie shell is commonly worn, in parts of South Africa, on the forehead in the region of the third eye.

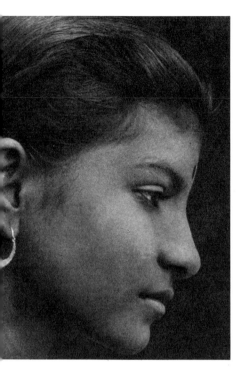

Caste mark on the forehead of an Indian girl.

Credo Mutwa, a Zulu *sangoma* in full regalia at initiation ceremony. On his head is a crown made from metal with a diamond shaped form over the area of the forehead and the location of the third eye. The diamond shape (see p. 51) is often used to symbolize the forces of the earth or the lower-self whose energies are gathered up into the forehead prior to their submission to the forces in the pineal area. Credo Mutwa, like many *sangoma,* sees the aura.

Initiation of a Swazi *sangoma* (witchdoctor). The bladders on the forehead of the apprentice sorceress or *twasa* have been taken from the sacrificial animal and contain one of the principal essences of life, the breath from her teacher (at left), which represents the Moya or Breath of Life. Another essence of life is the red ochre coating her hair.

The third eye

圖媾交虎龍

The third eye comes into manifestation as the energies of the soul, flowing through the Sahasrara or crown chakra and pineal, interact with the energies of the personality working through the Ajna chakra and the pituitary gland. Their blended fields form the Eye of Shiva – through this eye the soul can distinguish the divine light in all forms, and by focused attention can direct energies to drive out the lower elementals of earth, air, fire and water from the subtle bodies that form the personality, thus aiding in the purification of the lower-self. An ancient commentary puts it thus: 'One glance the soul doth cast upon the forms of mind. A ray of light streams out and darkness disappears; distortions and evil forms fade out, and all the little fires die out; the lesser lights are no more seen. The eye through light awakens into life the needed modes of Being. To the disciple this will carry knowledge. To the ignorant no sense is seen.'

Left-hand page:

The release of wisdom in the form of the goddess Minerva from the forehead of the philosopher, seen as Zeus, who reclines with the eagle, symbol of the soul, at his shoulder. In the background male and female figures embrace, signifying the fusion of the forces of the soul and personality. (Alchemical engraving from Michael Maier, *Atalanta Fugiens*, 1618.)

The Kalahari Bushman undergoes a form of initiation on his first hunting trip which involves the cutting of a circle of skin from the forehead of the animal he slays. An incision is then made in his own brow and the skin from the animal

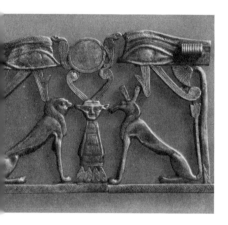

rubbed over it. The purpose of this ritual is to endow the hunter with superior sight to that of the animals he will hunt in the future. The acuity of the Bushmen's senses is legendary, and it is on record that many of them are able to see four of Jupiter's moons with the naked eye.

Legend has it that the gods destroyed the faculty of clairvoyance in man in order to force him to seek higher forms of spiritual perception. This pictorial script from Mexico is said to illustrate the legend, showing as it does a priest or god-like figure operating with a pointed instrument upon the forehead of a man. Those who erroneously consider clairvoyance to be a sign of high spiritual status may argue that this script in fact depicts the opening of the third eye. At

this point in the evolution of man, such an opening of inner vision would for many be a retrogressive step.

The energies issuing from the pineal and pituitary glands are symbolized by the tiger and the dragon, blending in the alchemical cauldron of the head to form the third eye. (Taoist illustration, China.)

Right-hand page:

Sculptures of the Buddha frequently depict the third eye on the forehead by a knob-like protuberance; in some cases a precious or semi-precious stone is set into the brow. (Gakko Bosatu, Nara, Japan, c. 8th c.)

The eye is often used as a symbol of God's Divine Awareness, and of the awakened intellectual and inner powers

of man. The Egyptians made full use of this symbol in their hieroglyphic writings and jewellery. (Electrum pectoral, Egypt, 20th–18th c. BC, Eton College, Windsor, England.)

The Seraph, covered with eyes even to the palms of his hands, illustrates the universal theme of the 'all-seeing eye'. As an Alaskan Eskimo song has it:

My whole body is covered with eyes:
Behold it! Be without fear!
I see all around.

(Detail of fresco by the Master of Pedret, Lérida, Spain, 11th c., Museo de Bellas Artes de Cataluña, Barcelona.)

Planes of consciousness

According to various esoteric schools, the Creation is divided into seven major planes of consciousness or matter. Man, made in the image of God, reflects this pattern through his manifestation upon the cosmic physical plane, and draws matter from the various levels in order to create bodies through which he can learn to express the Divinity which lies at the heart of his being. So common is this concept of gradations of consciousness and substance that references to it can be found in Christianity, Theosophy, Buddhism, Yoga, Judaism, Rosicrucianism, Sufism, as well as in the teachings of ancient Greece and Egypt. It is also to be found in the Zoroastrian religion and the spiritual beliefs of the Polynesians. An understanding of these inter-related planes of consciousness is basic to any study of the subtle anatomy of man.

This page:

A detailed outline of the energy complexes that constitute the occult anatomy of man. Here the lines of force linking the three aspects of the Monad can be traced from their source through the Spiritual Triad to the petals of the solar lotus, and outward through the chakras of the mental, astral and etheric bodies. To the man on the physical plane these lines are the Path by which he returns to his source. It is of interest to note that all of these force lines lead from the lower bodies and chakras to the higher, and from there to the Soul or centre of Christ consciousness, before going on to the Monad. We are thus reminded of Christ's saying that 'None cometh unto the Father but through me.' (The Egoic Lotus and the Centres, from Bailey, *Treatise on Cosmic Fire*.)

A modified version of the seven planes of consciousness, showing a symbolic interpretation of man's substance and perceptual structures.

The inner constitution of man and his fields of consciousness as used in psychosynthesis, a modern approach to the psychology of the total man which places a strong emphasis upon the integrating power of the Transpersonal or Higher Self. (Roberto Assagioli, *Psychosynthesis*, London 1971.)

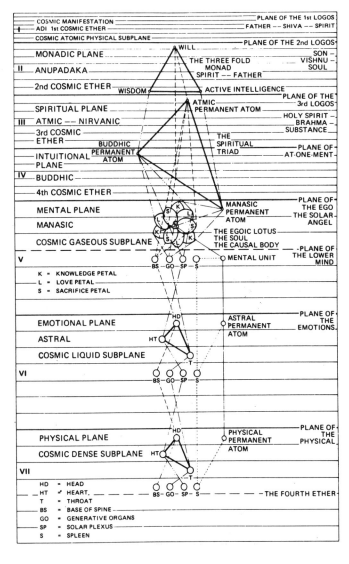

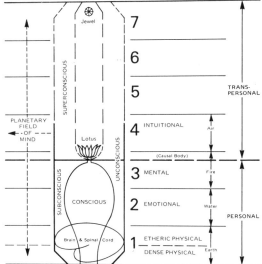

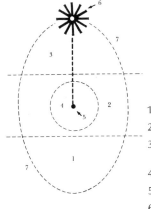

1 The Lower Unconscious
2 The Middle Unconscious
3 The Higher Unconscious, or Superconscious
4 The Field of Consciousness
5 The Conscious Self, or 'I'
6 The Transpersonal Self
7 The Collective Unconscious

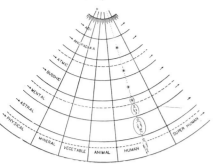

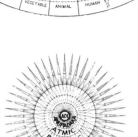

This page:

This chart shows the various levels upon which man has his being, and outlines the order of the kingdoms in nature through which the evolutionary progression of matter must pass. (The levels on which man lives, from I. K. Taimni, *Self-Culture*, London 1970.)

This diagram of the levels of consciousness illustrates the distinct 'separateness' inherent in the physical level of man, where the tips of the spikes are furthest from each other. As the spikes widen at the astral level they indicate less separation in consciousness. Only at the higher level of the mental plane (the soul level) do they begin to merge, and on the Buddhic level they overlap; here a true sense of union is experienced. (Unity in diversity, from Powell, *The Causal Body*.)

A Rosicrucian interpretation of the various levels of consciousness, or worlds, wherein man as a spiritual being functions. (*A Christian Rosenkreutz Anthology*, London 1968.)

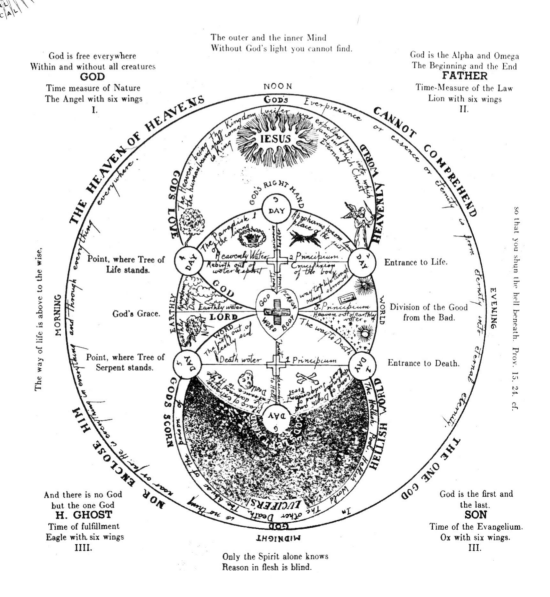

The Seven Major Spinal Chakras

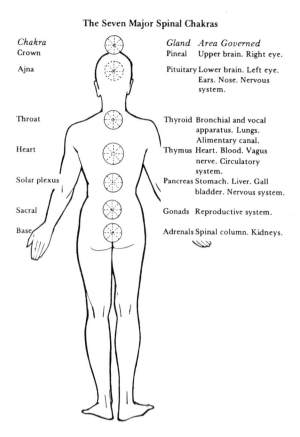

Chakra	Gland	Area Governed
Crown	Pineal	Upper brain. Right eye.
Ajna	Pituitary	Lower brain. Left eye. Ears. Nose. Nervous system.
Throat	Thyroid	Bronchial and vocal apparatus. Lungs. Alimentary canal.
Heart	Thymus	Heart. Blood. Vagus nerve. Circulatory system.
Solar plexus	Pancreas	Stomach. Liver. Gall bladder. Nervous system.
Sacral	Gonads	Reproductive system.
Base	Adrenals	Spinal column. Kidneys.

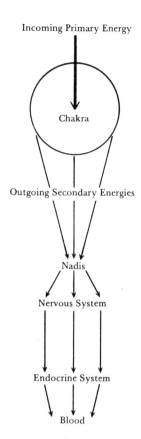

Incoming Primary Energy

Chakra

Outgoing Secondary Energies

Nadis

Nervous System

Endocrine System

Blood

Receptors and transmitters of energy

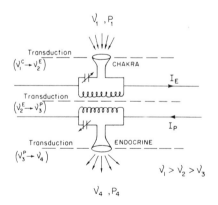

$$V_1, P_1$$

$$\text{Transduction} \left(V_1^C \rightarrow V_2^E \right) \qquad \text{CHAKRA}$$

$$I_E$$

$$\text{Transduction} \left(V_2^E \rightarrow V_3^P \right)$$

$$I_P$$

$$\text{Transduction} \left(V_3^P \rightarrow V_4 \right) \qquad \text{ENDOCRINE}$$

$$V_1 > V_2 > V_3$$

$$V_4, P_4$$

Through the chakras, the major nerve plexuses, the lesser ganglia and the intricate network of the fine nerves, man registers those energies and forces which flow to him from a multitude of sources throughout the universe, including the constellations of the zodiac and the planetary bodies. Similarly energies from the mental, emotional and etheric environment make their impress upon him, and as his spiritual unfoldment proceeds he becomes increasingly sensitive to the forces flowing to him from his soul, which are directed in such a manner as to galvanize the personality into fulfilling its purpose.

As well as acting as receivers of energy, the chakras also transmit energies for creative or destructive purposes. For example an individual who is strongly polarized in his astral body and working through an uncontrolled and highly developed solar plexus can create havoc one way or another in the environment where he functions. On the other hand a person who works creatively through the throat or the heart chakras radiates peace and harmony in such a way that

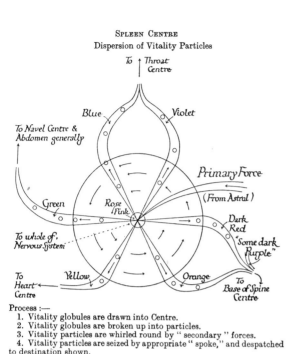

PRIMARY FORCE *(from Astral)*

Spleen Centre
Dispersion of Vitality Particles

To ↑ Throat Centre

Blue · Violet

To Navel Centre & Abdomen generally

Primary Force

(From Astral)

Green · Rose (Pink)

Dark Red

"Some dark Purple"

To whole of, Nervous System

To Heart Centre · Yellow · Orange

To Base of Spine Centre

Process :—
1. Vitality globules are drawn into Centre.
2. Vitality globules are broken up into particles.
3. Vitality particles are whirled round by " secondary " forces.
4. Vitality particles are seized by appropriate " spoke," and despatched to destination shown.

Violet from Throat Centre

Yellow from Heart Centre, giving power of high philosophical & metaphysical thought.

Appearance :
Central portion : " gleaming white, flushed with gold."
Outer portion : " most resplendent of all, full of indescribable chromatic effects."
Number of " spokes " : Central portion 12, outer portion 960.
Function of Astral Centre : perfects and completes faculties.
Function of Etheric Centre : gives continuity of consciousness.

others are uplifted and quietly inspired by its presence. By fulfilling the law through purification of the threefold lower-self and service to others the centres are slowly and automatically unfolded. By setting out deliberately to force the opening of the chakras, and to intensify their action, through chanting or other so-called spiritual exercises designed to raise the inner fires, the aspirant in his ignorance may unleash energies which will literally burn the physical tissues of his body, especially those of the nervous system and brain, thus leading to physical and emotional instability or at worst, insanity. In this way may be sown the seeds of prolonged trouble in future incarnations. The key that will open the centres lies quite simply in a steady orientation towards the soul and a responsiveness to soul contact expressed through service.

Left-hand page:

Each chakra externalizes as an endocrine gland and governs certain areas of the body. The healer will find in this chart a guide as to which areas of the body relate to the centres. In treatment the right hand can be used to introduce energy into the chakra while the left is held in the area of the physical organism where the problem lies. (The seven major spinal chakras, Tansley, *Radionics and the Subtle Anatomy of Man.*)

Energy flowing into a chakra and through the organism should ideally find expression outwards upon the physical plane; inhibition of flow ultimately leads to disease. If a chakra has been damaged by physical or emotional shock then reception and distribution of energy may be impaired, with consequent dysfunction in the area of the body governed by that centre. For example, emotional shock damaging the throat chakra may give rise to asthma; or, if the solar plexus centre is disabled in a similar way, then diabetes may appear. Clearly, if the chakra can be returned to a state of balance then the physical organism will follow and health will ensue. For a correct flow of energy the various aspects of the physical and subtle bodies must be well coordinated. Frequently a poor or loose connection between the nadis and the nervous system will result in chronic fatigue. (Energy flow through a chakra, Tansley, *Radionics and the Subtle Anatomy of Man.*)

A modern interpretation of the relationship and energy flow between a chakra and an endocrine gland. (William Tiller, *Radionics, Radiesthesia and Physics.*)

This page:

The vitalizing energy of the sun is absorbed by the spleen chakra and distributed by way of the etheric body to the physical form. (Spleen centre, from Powell, *The Etheric Double.*)

The reception and distribution of energy in the crown chakra according to C. W. Leadbeater. (Top-of-head centre, from Powell, *The Etheric Double.*)

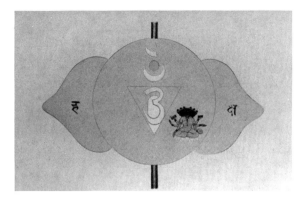

The Ajna or brow chakra.

Symbols of the chakras

Traditional Indian teachings depict the chakras with a mandala-like design in the form of a wheel or flower. The circle contains a Sanskrit inscription representing the fundamental or primary note of the centre; and with it a symbolic animal such as an elephant or antelope may be shown along with a god or goddess. The animals signify the character of the forces that manifest in the chakra; and the gods and goddesses symbolize the divine energies of a higher nature that accompany them. The circle is surrounded by a varying number of petals; upon each petal is a Sanskrit syllable representing a particular frequency or mystic sound which corresponds to the harmonics of the primary note at the centre of the wheel. The petals are seen as an expression of force and its apparent effect in matter.

Biblical writings use the symbol of the wheel or seal to represent the force centres or chakras in the subtle bodies of man, and it is significant that St John places these seals upon the back of the book of life, and not on the front as an astral psychic would see them. Each of the Churches of the Book of Revelation is said to be analogous to one of the seven major spinal chakras: the Church

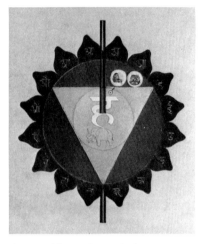

The Visuddha or throat chakra.

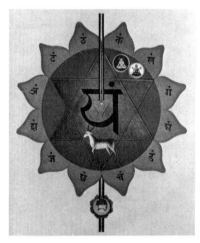

The Anahata or heart chakra.

The Manipura or solar plexus chakra.

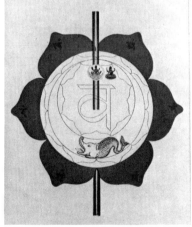

The Svadhisthana or sacral chakra.

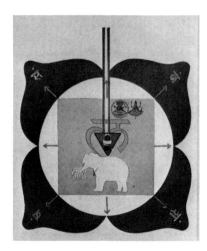

The muladhara or base chakra.

of Ephesus representing the base chakra, the Church of Pergamos the sacral, the Church of Smyrna the solar plexus, the Church of Thyatira the heart, the Church of Sardis the throat, the Church of Philadelphia the brow and the Church of Laodicea the crown centre.

There are a total of forty-eight petals in the five lower chakras; and when these are synthesized into the two-petalled lotus of the Ajna centre the number fifty arises, which is the number of the perfected personality. If the ninety-six component petals of the two divisions of the Ajna are added to the forty-eight petals of the five lower centres, the total is one hundred and forty-four. This number represents the completion of the work which brings the lower-self into perfect union with the soul. Follow the one hundred and forty-four with the one thousand petals of the crown chakra, and you have the number of the saved in the Book of Revelation. One hundred and forty-four thousand symbolizes the complete transformation of the individual who can then stand before the Presence Itself.

Left-hand page:

Symbols of the chakras. (Sir John Wood-roffe, *The Serpent Power*, Madras 1972.)

This page:

There are probably any number of interpretations to the Book of Revelation, for like any true esoteric document it can be the key to knowledge in a variety of fields. For those who heed the admonition of the Delphic oracle, 'Know Thyself', Revelation is a textbook of the subtle anatomy of man, filled with information on the various bodies of the personality, the soul and the spirit and of course the chakras. (Rosicrucian illustration of the seven seals, *A Christian Rosenkreutz Anthology*.)

In this illustration of the seven major chakras they are depicted as lotus blooms, but no attempt has been made to put in the correct number of petals to each centre. It does show however the reflection of the Spiritual Triad in the

lower-self, which works with the energies of Love through the heart centre, Intelligence through the throat centre and Will through the crown centre. The personality works through a lower series of chakras: the solar plexus, the sacral and the base. In the process of evolving, man transfers the energies of the base chakra to the crown, the energies of the sacral to the throat and those of the solar plexus to the heart. In this way the physical will-to-be at the base is absorbed in the spiritual will-to-be at the crown. The energies of procreation are lifted to the higher creative centre at the throat, and the selfish individual drives and desires of the solar plexus are transmuted into group consciousness in the heart. (Bailey, *Esoteric Healing.*)

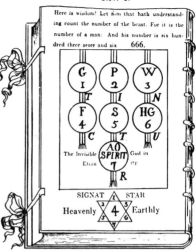

The Sealed Book.
Rev. 5.

REFLECTION OF THE SPIRITUAL TRIAD IN THE PERSONALITY

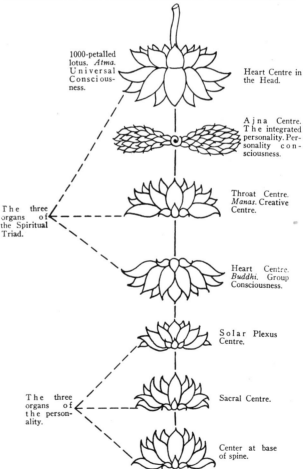

away the protective etheric webs which lie along the spine between the chakras. The raising of Kundalini can only come about safely when the Monad, through the power of directed thought, has control over the vehicles of the lower-self. Those who attempt to arouse this energy before they have reached an advanced point in evolution are destined through their own ignorance to failure. This is frequently accompanied by deep psychological and physical disturbances. C. G. Jung stressed the dangers to those in the western world who embrace specific eastern techniques of spiritual development. He did so because eastern man is characterized by *tamas* or inertia (which is particularly evident in India), and western man by *rajas* or striving activity. The spiritual exercises that come out of India are designed to arouse the aspirant to activity and to stimulate him. Obviously, when a western student practises such exercises with diligence he is courting disaster in the form of an overstimulation of his inner nature, which in our present society displays a surfeit of striving.

The psychic nature of man is portrayed here, with its positive and negative aspects on the right and left sides of the body. Around the head is the telepathic aura which holds the serpents of wisdom enthralled. Between the serpents is the heart of universal awareness and love and at the solar plexus lies a smaller snake symbolizing psychic abilities. Upon the right hand, a scorpion indicates locked-in wisdom and destructive forces combined. Over the physical heart, four hearts symbolize empathy and compassion multiplied four-fold. (Command of Power, painting by Ingo Swann, USA, 1964.)

The symbol of the Orphic Mysteries is the serpent, representing the fiery Creative Spirit, wound around the egg which signifies the Cosmos. The egg may also symbolize the soul of the philosopher and the snake the Mystery teachings. (The Orphic Egg, after J. Bryant, *An Analysis of Ancient Mythology*, 1774.)

The snake as a symbol of spiritual power

The snake is found as a symbol of regenerative spiritual energies in virtually all teachings, and in particular in those of India. The Kundalini power, as it is called, is the great primary force that energizes all forms. In man it is described as a mystic fire, electrical in nature, that lies coiled at the base of the spine. When aroused it rises up the etheric spine in a spiralling movement, burning

In Africa, as in many other lands, the snake is looked upon as a symbol of power. Tradition has it that earth tremors are created by the spirit snake as it moves about its underground domain; early African miners sacrificed animals to placate this deity before they began any mining operations. Anthropologist, archaeologist and museum director Adrian Boshier arrived in South Africa from England when he was sixteen. Drawn to the Bush, he spent ten years roaming on foot, sleeping in caves and living off the land. His search for knowledge inevitably led him to the witchdoctors of various tribes. With his capacity to handle venomous snakes it is not surprising that, at his initiation as a *sangoma*, his headband bears a snake motif, and a metal snake symbolizing spiritual power and guidance is entwined around his right arm.

The highly magnetized snake on the head of the Pharaoh was placed so that its tail touched the medulla and drew the fiery energies of the spine into the pituitary body and then upward to the pineal gland. Its purpose was to keep the psychic forces sublimated to the higher chakras. (Head of Amenophis III, relief, Thebes, Egypt, c. 1380 BC, Staatliche Museen, Berlin.)

The spiritual power symbolized by the snake is seen here winding itself around the column to come face to face with St Simon Stylites who sits in meditation. (Gold plaque, Syria, 6th c., Louvre, Paris.)

The soul

A mandala symbolizes the soul of man as a circular movement around a central point of concentrated spiritual power. It is depicted in some teachings as a lotus, the petals of which symbolize specific types of constituent energies. Taoist writers have referred to it as the Golden Flower, to indicate the quality of its sun-like radiance; and Jacob Boehme called it the 'philosophical eye'. The mystic often experiences his soul in terms of light, and this is most graphically expressed by St Gregory Palamas, who wrote of the Apostle's vision: 'Paul saw a light without limits below or above or to the sides; he saw no limit whatever to the light that appeared to him and shone around him, but it was like a sun infinitely brighter and vaster than the universe; and in the midst of this sun he himself stood, having become nothing but eye.'

The soul then may be seen and experienced as a unit of light, the radiance of which is unveiled as the bodies of the lower-self are brought to such a state of purity and transparency that nothing hinders the outflow of light.

This page:

In this painting, inspired by Christian teachings, the soul is depicted as a child-like figure of innocence being carried upwards by two angelic beings towards God. The Deity is shown as the central point of a mandala of light surrounded by twelve angels. (The Soul of St Bertin carried up to God, painting by Simon Marmion, France, 15th c., National Gallery, London.)

The weighing of the soul against a feather may be more literal than symbolic. Certain esoteric schools teach that the specific gravity of the soul increases in proportion to the feedback of meritorious living from each incarnation. It has also been clinically observed that at the instant of death when the inner bodies are withdrawn from the physical form, there is a measurable reduction in the weight of the individual. (Weighing the soul, from Book of the Dead, papyrus, Egypt, c. 1450 BC, British Museum, London.)

Right-hand page:

Here in diagrammatic form is the mandala of the soul showing the twelve petals around a central point of energy, often called the Jewel in the Lotus. The three outer petals are those of the energies of Active Intelligence; next come the petals of love, which relate to the Love-wisdom aspect of the Monad; and between these and the three which enfold the central jewel lie the petals of sacrifice or Will. The vehicle of the soul on the levels of the abstract mind is called the causal body and corresponds symbolically to the upper room where the disciples sat with Christ at the Last Supper. The twelve petals around the central point of dynamic energy are analogous to the disciples gathering around the Christ. The three inner petals, which for aeons were folded like a bud over the focal point of energy, do not unfold until the later stages of the Path are being trod; they symbolize for us the physical, astral and mental bodies of man, in the persons of Peter, James and John, who were capable of being present at the Transfiguration. The twelve petals are also seen to be analogous to the twelve signs of the zodiac, which cover the sum total of experience that man must build into his soul, and to the twelve foundation stones and twelve gates of the City of Peace. Perhaps, too, the twelve cranial nerves are directly related to the various energies of the soul. The diagram also shows another and most vital factor in the subtle anatomy of man: this is the Antaskarana or rainbow bridge which links the personality directly to the Monad by way of the Spiritual Triad. This structure, known as Jacob's Ladder in the Bible, is built through the cooperative efforts of the soul and the personality for the purpose of bridging the definite gap that exists in consciousness between the levels of the concrete and abstract minds. A useful physiological analogy is the synaptic cleft: the gap that exists between the dendrites of two neurons in the nervous system. In our bodies the nerve impulse bridges that gap through a chemical reaction, whereas in the totality of our being the gap is bridged by an inner alchemy stimulated by meditation and the clear intent to serve. (The Egoic Lotus, Bailey, *Treatise on Cosmic Fire*.)

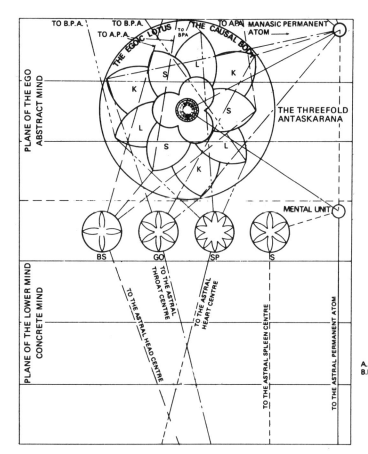

PLANE OF THE EGO
ABSTRACT MIND

TO B.P.A.   TO B.P.A.   TO APA   MANASIC PERMANENT
      TO A.P.A.   TO APA   ATOM →
                   THE EGOIC LOTUS   TO   THE CAUSAL BODY
                                      BPA

THE THREEFOLD
ANTASKARANA

MENTAL UNIT

BS   GO   SP   S

PLANE OF THE LOWER MIND
CONCRETE MIND

TO THE ASTRAL HEAD CENTRE
TO THE ASTRAL THROAT CENTRE
TO THE ASTRAL HEART CENTRE
TO THE ASTRAL SPLEEN CENTRE
TO THE ASTRAL PERMANENT ATOM

A.P.A. = ATMIC PERMANENT ATOM
B.P.A. = BUDDHIC PERMANENT ATOM

K = KNOWLEDGE PETAL
L = LOVE PETAL
S = SACRIFICE PETAL

BS = BASE OF SPINE
GO = GENERATIVE ORGANS
SP = SOLAR PLEXUS
S = SPLEEN

Whereas the aura of the lower-self presents a constant shifting series of colours and patterns, the archetype or sound pattern of the soul, while vitally alive, remains unchanged during incarnation. Changes take place in the pattern of the archetype between death and rebirth, as the good, creative and constructive essences of the past life are built into it. These unique paintings were made by an artist who had the capacity to observe such phenomena at the soul level. To the initiate with the power to read the meaning of the symbols contained in the patterns of the archetype, the nature of the soul is immediately revealed. (Archetypes of Sir Winston Churchill and Mme Chiang Kai-Shek, paintings by Nancy Lonsdale from Heline, *The Archetype Unveiled*.)

Meditation and prayer

Through prayer and meditation man aligns his lower-self to the soul and ultimately to the spirit within. In so doing he learns through persistence, love and patience to recognize and control the psychic forces of consciousness, to withhold energy from the negative and destructive tendencies of the lower-self, and to enhance and develop the constructive qualities. Through this process, carried on over many incarnations, each of the bodies of the personality is purified and oriented towards the inner spiritual reality; thus man in the three worlds becomes a fitting channel of expression for the purpose of the soul. Many teachers recommend the repetition of the Divine name or a mantram to bring about concentration and stillness of the mind, others teach that constant visualization of certain symbols will lead to union with God. Whatever methods are used, it finally becomes clear to the aspirant that he must pierce the form of his spiritual exercises to the reality beyond. Meister Eckhart stressed this when he wrote: 'He who seeks God under settled form lays hold of the form, while missing the God concealed in it.'

It is common practice for the mystic to seek solitude to deepen his communion with God. Many, like St Simon Stylites, have chosen to sit in isolation on top of a pole to carry out their prayers and meditation. (St. Alypios the Stylite, icon by Constantine Cantoris, Corfu, 1716.)

To pray, it has been said, is to stand before God in order to enter into a direct and personal relationship with Him. It is not so much an activity at specific times as an entering into the stillness with an attitude of positive alertness and a continuous state of awareness on the highest level of consciousness one can reach. A Syrian monk, Isaac of Niniveh, wrote: 'Every man who delights in a multitude of words, even when he says admirable things, is empty within. If you love truth, be a lover of silence. Silence like the sunlight will illuminate you in God and will deliver you from the phantoms of ignorance.' (Fr Antonio in prayer, Serra San Bruno, Italy.)

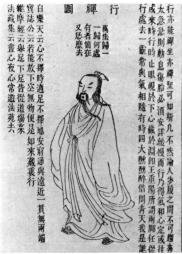

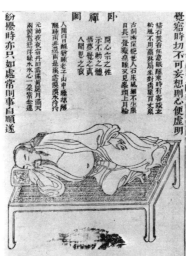

Those who are well versed in the art of meditation can maintain a high level of conscious awareness of their inner work while going about their daily business. It is eventually possible to reach a continuity of consciousness throughout both waking and sleeping states. The adept is conscious of what he is doing, in or out of the physical body, twenty-four hours a day. Eventually he moves with equal awareness and facility through the cycles of life and death, maintaining this continuity of consciousness. (Meditation standing, sitting, walking and lying down, book illustrations, China, Bibliothèque Nationale, Paris.)

Meditation is the path by which one withdraws from the peripheral stresses and storms of the personality to the centre of calm and tranquillity that lies within. The wise man reverts his sight and looks inward towards the light of immortality.

The path of initiation

As a man evolves, he passes from one state of consciousness to another. The final stages of his journey are frequently referred to as the path of initiation, which most religions divide into five stages or points of crisis. Nowhere was this more clearly illustrated for man than in the life of Jesus Christ, where each initiation was preceded by a journey, symbolizing the treading of the Path. The first initiation, represented by the Nativity in the stable or cave at Bethlehem, symbolizes the birth of the Christ within the heart of the individual who has now been summoned by his soul to a new life. The second initiation, the Baptism in Jordan, indicates the culmination of purification of the lower-self and its readiness to enter a cycle of intense outer activity. The third initiation symbolizes the submission of the lower nature to the purpose of the soul – 'and his face did shine as the sun (soul), and his raiment (aura) was white as the light'. At this initiation Peter, James and John symbolize the physical, astral and mental aspects of His human nature, positioned just below the peak of the Mount of Transfiguration. At the fourth initiation, the Crucifixion, Christ symbolizes the cosmic spirit crucified upon the cross of matter, and hanging between heaven and earth. He clearly shows his role as mediator between these two aspects of creation as he founds the Kingdom of Heaven upon earth. The fifth initiation is divided into two halves, the Resurrection and the Ascension. In the former Christ demonstrates that death can be overcome when divinity is fully expressed through the human form. His Ascension marks the culmination of the drama of consciousness, unfolded and fulfilled for all men to see and emulate.

Left-hand page :

The Mystic Nativity, painting by Sandro Botticelli, Italy, 15th c., National Gallery, London.

The Baptism of Christ, painting by Piero della Francesca, Italy, 15th c., National Gallery, London.

The Transfiguration, painting by Fra Angelico, Italy, 15th c., San Marco, Florence.

This page :

The Crucifixion, painting by Antonello da Messina, Italy, 15th c., National Gallery, London.

The Resurrection, painting by Ugolino di Nerio, Italy, 14th c., National Gallery, London.

The Ascension, painting by Orcagna, Italy, 14th c., National Gallery, London.

The quantum leap in consciousness

Enlightenment is not a step-by-step process but a sudden leap. This movement from one state of consciousness to another seems frequently to be characterized by two primary factors, one of acute inner tension and spiritual anguish followed by a sudden and often dramatic release or surrender of the personality to a higher aspect of consciousness. If properly utilized, meditation and prayer serve to heighten the tension at such times. Another device is the Zen *koan* that corners the intellectual mind with a problem it cannot solve through the normal thinking processes. Don Juan and Don Genaro, whispering simultaneously into the ears of Castaneda, create an acute condition of inner tension in order to precipitate him into a state of expanded awareness. The Indian saint Sri Ramakrishna, in complete desperation, leapt from his meditations and tore a sword from the temple wall to kill himself – at that instant he reached enlightenment. Don Juan speaks of the 'crack between the worlds' as a doorway beyond which lies the abyss.

To the Zulu this point beyond time and space is the 'gate of distance'. The *Upanishads* say: 'Where heaven and earth meet there is a space wide as a razor's edge or a fly's wing through which one may pass to another world.'

The aspirant to wisdom passes through the doorway of initiation from the everyday consciousness of the lower-self to another world of heightened awareness. Following this he is never the same, nor is his view of the world. The leap from one state or world to another involves a self-naughting, a hurling of one's self into the void of Creation, into a state of imagelessness. It means, as Benet of Caulfield says, to live in the abyss of the Divine Essence, to return to the nothingness of things by annihilation; thus the personality of man symbolically dies to the soul of Christ consciousness within, and paradoxically, out of nothingness and annihilation, emerges in all his fullness as the New Man. Jesus, like the Masters of Zen Buddhism, points out that we can move instantaneously into this world of expanded consciousness simply through recognition of The

94

Presence. 'If ye be in the Spirit, ye are no more under the law', said Jesus; and he spoke of the law of the illusions and limitations of human beliefs and thinking. The Zen Master would say that you are already enlightened, it's just that you don't realize it. 'Set yourself and see,' said Jesus: turn from the illusory world you live in, 'see' the world of reality and be governed by it now, step into the void of the consciousness of Spirit, for in the void lies the fullness of all Creation.

Although external aids such as drugs may provide the illusion of expanded spiritual awareness, they do untold damage to the subtle and luminous bodies. Man, by his own efforts, must find his way, guided by the teachings of the past and harkening to his inner voice. The *Lankavatra sutra* points out that by concentrating the thoughts or energies of the mental body one can fly and be born in heaven. A Chinese text says, 'Silently in the morning thou fliest upwards.' Concentrating the desires or energies of the astral body, it seems, causes one to fall. (Dreaming of Immortality in a thatched cottage, screen, probably by Chou Ch'en, China, 16th c., Smithsonian Institute, Freer Gallery of Art, Washington, D C.)

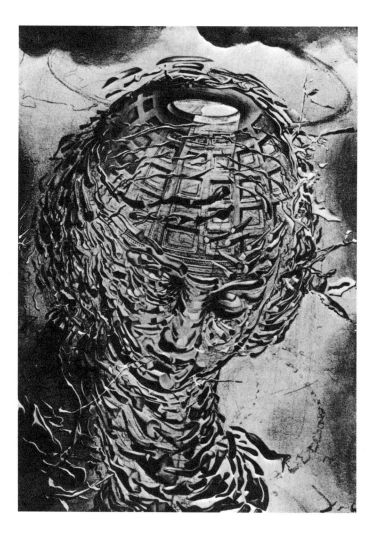

Artist Yves Klein, shown here in the act of literally leaping into 'the Void' in a physical exploration of space, risking serious injury or even death in order to attempt to capture the sensation that accompanies this leap on the higher levels of consciousness. (Leap into the Void, action by Yves Klein, France, 1961.)

As the aspirant symbolically stands on the edge of the abyss looking into the void, he knows that his personality faces absorption into the infinite, and he feels quite frequently that a fragmentation of his being will take place. In *Tales of Power*, Castaneda captures the essence of this experience when he speaks of his descent moving back and forth like a leaf dropping and his head being stripped of all its weight. All of his being, concentrated at one point, seemed to burst into a thousand pieces; yet he was awareness itself. (Fragmented head after Raphael, painting by Salvador Dali, Spain, 1951, Private Collection, England.)

Sources and further reading

Bailey, Alice A., *Treatise on Cosmic Fire*, London and New York 1962; *Telepathy and the Etheric Vehicle*, London and New York 1957; *Esoteric Healing*, London and New York 1953; *Letters on Occult Meditation*, London and New York 1974.

Besant, Annie, *Man and his Bodies*, Madras 1960.

Boehme, Jacob, *The Aurora*, London 1960.

Carlson, Rick, *The Frontiers of Science and Medicine*, London 1975.

Castaneda, Carlos, *The Teachings of Don Juan*, Berkeley 1968 and London 1970; *A Separate Reality*, London and New York 1971; *Journey to Ixtlan*, London and New York 1972; *Tales of Power*, London and New York 1974.

Chang, Chung-Yuan, *Creativity of Taoism*, London 1975.

Deussen, P., *The Philosophy of the Upanishads*, New York 1966.

Hall, Manly Palmer, *Man, Grand Symbol of the Mysteries*, Los Angeles, Calif., 1947.

Heindel, Max, *The Vital Body*, Oceanside, Calif., 1950.

Heline, Corinne, *Occult Anatomy and the Bible*, Oceanside, Calif., 1940.

Heline, Theodore, *The Archetype Unveiled*, Oceanside, Calif., 1965.

Karagulla, Shafica, *Breakthrough to Creativity*, Santa Monica, Calif., 1967.

Kilner, Walter, *The Human Aura*, New York 1965.

Leadbeater, C. W., *Man Visible and Invisible*, Wheaton, Ill., and London 1969; *The Chakras*, Wheaton, Ill., and London 1972.

Mead, G. R. S., *The Doctrine of the Subtle Body*, Wheaton, Ill., and London 1967.

Milner, D. and E. Smart, *The Loom of Creation*, London 1976.

Powell, A. E., *The Etheric Double*, London 1960; *The Astral Body*, London 1965; *The Mental Body*, Wheaton, Ill., and London 1956; *The Causal Body*, Wheaton, Ill., and London 1956.

Regush, Nicholas, *The Human Aura*, Englefield Cliffs, N.J., 1975.

Rele, V., *The Mysterious Kundalini*, India 1967.

Roberts, Jane, *The Nature of Personal Reality*, Englefield Cliffs, N.J., 1974.

Scott, Mary, *Science and Subtle Bodies*, London 1975.

Steiner, Rudolf, *An Occult Physiology*, London n.d.

Tansley, David V., *Radionics and the Subtle Anatomy of Man*, Bradford, Devon, 1972; *Radionics – Interface with the Ether Fields*, Bradford, Devon, 1975.

Ware, Archimandrite Kallistos, *The Power of The Name: the Jesus Prayer in Orthodox Spirituality*, London 1974.

Wilhelm, Richard, ed., *Secret of the Golden Flower*, New York and London 1962.

Woodroffe, Sir John, *The Serpent Power*, Madras 1972.

Acknowledgments

The objects in the plates, pp. 33–64, are in the collections of Bremen, Kunsthalle 40; Colmar, Musée Unterlinden 48; Glasgow, Art Gallery 64; Istanbul, Topkapi Saray Museum 33; Johannesburg, Museum of Man and Science 51; Kyoto, Jingo-ji 49; London, National Gallery 53, 61; New York, Pierpont Morgan Library 41; Paris, Bibliothèque Nationale 34; Philadelphia, Museum of Art 43; Prague, Narodni Galerie 39; Stockholm, National Museum 60; Washington, Smithsonian Institution, Freer Gallery of Art 38.

Photographs were supplied by Camera Press 71, 74, 76; Provost and Fellows, Eton 79 below; Mary Evans Picture Library 68 below: Galerie Karl Flinker 45; Louis Fourie 69 r.; Jeremy Grayson 91 below; George G. Harrap & Co. Ltd. 57; Health Science Press 70 l., 82 above (2); Pierre Hinch 76 r., 77 below (2); Hutchinson Publishing Group Ltd. 37; Manly Palmer Hall, Philosophical Research Society 36, 56; Japan Publication Inc. 69 r., Richard Lannoy 77 above; Lucis Press 19, 80 l., 85 below, 89 above; Mansell Collection 62–3, 88 below; Marlborough Gallery, New York 55; Mas 79 r.; Methuen & Co. 54; Rex Features 65; Editions du Seuil 34; H. Shunk 94 below; Rudolph Steiner Publications 50, 81 below, 85 above; Theosophical Publishing House 31, 52, 81 above (2), 83 (2); Reprinted by permission of University Books Inc. 19, 30, 67 above (2), centre; Reprinted by permission of Viking Penguin Inc. 80 below r., John Webb 53, 61; Samuel Weiser Inc. 24, 42; Wildwood House Ltd. 58, 59.